JESUSChicks

SARAH BOWLING

SAVING MOSES®
saving babies every day

savingmoses.org
PO Box 4584 • Englewood, CO 80155-9964

Jesus Chicks
by Sarah Bowling

Copyright © 2015

PO Box 4584
Englewood, CO 80155-9964
1.888.637.4545

ISBN# 978-1-938696-64-0

All proceeds from the sale of this book will go to Saving Moses.
Saving Moses is a global humanitarian organization saving
babies (5 & under) every day by meeting the most urgent
needs where care is least available.

savingmoses.org
saving babies every day

Printed in the United States of America

Unless otherwise indicated, all Scripture quotations are
taken from the New King James Version of the Bible.

CONTENTS

INTRODUCTION

Women have a unique predisposition to connect along relational lines. Men tend to connect through work and activity but women connect through conversation and on different emotional levels. We like to talk over coffee; we like book clubs; we join zumba groups; we enjoy our friends on Facebook and much more.

When we think about Jesus' followers, we frequently default to Peter, James, and John, along with the other nine men whom Jesus selected to be His apostles or close followers. These men followed Jesus for around three years and as we read through the Gospels, we learn a lot about these men and even more about Jesus from their interactions with Him.

In the Gospels, we're also given some really unique perspectives on Jesus based on His interactions with women. I've written this book to help each reader connect with Jesus in a powerful, relevant, and daily way.

CHAPTER 1
RELATIONSHIPS
Samaritan Woman

Have you ever experienced relationship failure? Several years ago, one of my central friendships completely hit the fan with lots of bleeding heart splattered everywhere. It was u-g-l-y, ugly and painful for a very long time. When I say a long time, I'm talking more than ten years of ugly. But it was interesting to watch God work in that relationship, change me, grow me, and help me to make some very important adjustments. That particular friendship had been through some dysfunction and God started to really work on those things in my heart. After more than ten years, my friend and I met up to talk through some of the challenges that we had and after some time and constructive conversations, this friendship has been restored and it's a wonderful, wonderful testimony to the goodness, love, and transforming power of God!

As women, one of the central values in our lives is relationships. Relationships are so important to us that often our sense of value can rise or fall based on how things are going in our various relationships —be that our marriage, with our kids or parents, friendships, work or school connections, etc. As a woman, relationships are a big deal to us in small, medium, and big ways. If you think about it, women are the ones who are most frequently found in book clubs, work-out classes, going to the bathroom in groups, and participating in various small groups. Women's ministries at churches are stereotypically larger and often more dynamic than their male counterparts. Relationships are important to women. So when a woman isolates and detaches herself from relationships and normal, healthy and daily connections, it's often a red flag that something isn't going right. Most often, something has gone tragically wrong and there's pain in this person's heart.

We've all had failure in relationships. Whether that's through a divorce or maybe a friendship that's been seemingly lost, there's irreparable damage. Often times, things are said that shouldn't have been said and a lot of hurt can linger in a person's heart from painful conversations and even painful silence. But what seems like failure can also be the starting point for redemption.

Let's consider the dialogue that happens between a very broken woman and Jesus in John 4. In this chapter, we see that there's a woman who has experienced failure after failure after failure and many broken relationships—and she struggled. She wanted healthy intimacy, like all of us. We want closeness and there's nothing wrong with that because that's how we are wired up by God. We are designed to have healthy friendships and relationships. But the woman in John 4 experienced one train wreck after another, and she was living in that failure.

And maybe that's you today. Maybe you're living in failed relationship after failed relationship after failed relationship. I want to speak hope into your life that God can redeem that, can transform that, and bring you out and through to tremendous victory. That's what we see in John Chapter 4. And so when we think about this woman, let me give you some context.

In John 4, we meet a woman who was a Samaritan. In the beginning of the chapter, we read that Jesus *needed* to go through Samaria. What's the big deal about Samaria? Let me walk you through just a little bit of historical background so you can understand some of the surroundings and the context of what's happening between Jesus and this woman. First of all, you recall, Jesus is Jewish and he's going through Samaria. Samaria and the Jews didn't really have a good relationship between them. Samaritans usually did not like the Jews. And the Jews looked down on the Samaritans, seeing them as second class, at best. So there was already cultural conflict between these two ethnicities. And when the Bible says, "He needed to go through Samaria," this is noteworthy because He could have gone around. He could have avoided Samaria and it was very common for most religious and proper Jews to avoid Samaria, so they didn't get tainted or corrupted by the "yucky" Samaritan second class people. But Jesus didn't do that. He went through Samaria - even *needing* to go through Samaria.

Furthermore, at this time in history, men and women didn't really talk to each other unless they, of course, were married. If this was a foreign woman or a stranger, and Jesus had never met her, it would be completely inappropriate and culturally unacceptable for Him to talk to her and for her to talk with Him.

And when He starts into Samaria, John 4:6 says that Jesus was tired from His journey, so He sat down next to a well around noontime or so. His disciples had gone into the nearby city to get some lunch. But it's important to consider that at this time in history, the water wells were oftentimes at the outskirts of a city or a town for hygienic reasons. So Jesus being tired from the journey sat down by this well, on the outskirts of a Samaritan city around noontime or so.

As He's sitting by the well, a woman comes to draw water from the well and this is a really interesting time for this woman to come and draw water. Normally in this culture, the women would come and draw the water either in the morning to have water for the day, or in the evening to get water for the night. They also went in the morning or the evening because you would avoid the heat of the day. Now when you think about it, we women tend to do everything at least with a couple friends. We go for coffee. We go to the bathroom together. We talk with each other on the phone while we shop. We message each other on Facebook, text a friend while we wait to pick up our kids from school, tweet our friends about a homework assignment and lots more. Generally, we're very social because that's how we're wired up.

So when this woman comes to draw water at noon, something is shady. Things get even more dicey when she comes to the well and a Jewish man is sitting at the well. Let's take an account of what's strange in this picture thus far.

- *First of all there's Jesus, a Jewish man going through Samaria —that normally shouldn't happen*

- *This Samaritan woman comes to the well at noon —a very unusual time*

- *This same Samaritan woman is drawing water alone—consider that most women look for opportunities to socialize or hang out and chat rather than looking for ways to isolate, hide, or withdraw*

These are three strange things and if you think about it, when we are broken in our relationships, we do strange things. We sometimes act abnormally, isolate, and withdraw. But if you find yourself doing some of this stuff because you have some broken relationships, Jesus wants to help you, just like He did with this Samaritan woman. Jesus comes to you, passing beyond the social and cultural norms to connect with you —even in your brokenness, pain, and hurt. Jesus comes to us to bring redemption and to mend that which has been broken and dysfunctional.

So Jesus jumps over all the cultural and social norms and asks this lady for a drink of water because He has something way bigger in mind than merely a drink of water. Don't ever think that what seems as common as a drink of water can't become something extraordinary and miraculous with Jesus. You can tell by her reaction that this Samaritan woman is blown away by Jesus' request for a drink of water.

In John 4:9 she immediately says what is culturally acceptable, saying, "How is it that you, a Jew, ask a drink of water from me, a Samaritan woman." Basically, she's saying, "You shouldn't be talking with me! You are violating all the cultural norms." But one of the things that is so entirely cool about Jesus is that He defies all cultural norms. And I love that He initiates this conversation. It wasn't the woman who started the discussion. It was Jesus coming into her world, coming into her brokenness, coming into her state of failure and really speaking into that and initiating the relationship. And that's what Jesus does with us. He initiates the relationship with us. Number one, because He loves us. Number two, because He wants to repair, redeem, and restore us so that we can have healthy relationships and healthy intimacy.

So this broken and dysfunctional Samaritan woman starts to talk with Jesus, a Jewish man sitting by a water well, so common and daily but incarnate. If she only knew with whom she was speaking. "How is it that you, a Jew, a Jewish man, speak with me, a Samaritan woman?" Jesus keeps the conversation going, drawing her into an increasingly deeper conversation. He just doesn't tell her, "shut up lady and give me some water". Jesus doesn't do that because that's not who Jesus is. He's the personification of love, relationship, and connection - wanting to have a deep, healthy, and vibrant relationship with us. So He starts talking with her and He says, "If you knew who it was that was asking you for a drink of water, you would ask me and I would give you living water."

And thus begins the process Jesus uses to transform this amazing and wonderful Samaritan woman - all starting with Jesus asking her for a drink of water. As the conversation progresses, she asks Jesus, "Well how is it that you can give me living water? You don't have anything to draw water with." So this conversation continues to go even deeper, to develop, grow and unfold...and it seems to me that this Samaritan woman is enjoying it. Clearly, Jesus is talking with her because He's interested in who she is, not just what she can do for Him. And that speaks to the very core of what is sometimes so very wrong in our hearts. So many times in our lives we struggle because we've been used. We've been used as an object. We've been mistreated. And truthfully, God has really dealt with me on this. Sometimes when we treat other people as objects or we use other people, that hurts us. In Proverbs 1:19 it says, when you hurt someone else, it hurts you. You can't hurt somebody else without hurting yourself.

Despite the questions from the Samaritan woman, what Jesus does next absolutely takes your breath away. Jesus and this Samaritan woman are having this beautiful and enjoyable conversation and Jesus throws a massive monkey wrench in the whole discussion. He makes the entire conversation explode and go nuclear because He goes to the very heart of what her issue is. He says in John 4:16 "Go and call your husband." And the Samaritan woman, who has been so conversational up to this point with this really cool Jewish guy, suddenly becomes extremely abrupt. There is a sudden and dramatic halt to the discussion. And she says, "I don't have a husband."

What Jesus did was hit the rawest nerve He could possibly touch in this woman. And this is one of the things that I love about Jesus. When Jesus started this conversation, He's Jesus Christ. He's the Son of God. He knows all things from the beginning to the end. He knows who this woman is. He knows He's going to sit down and ask her for a drink of water. He knows how the conversation's going to go. He knows all of her background. He knows who she is, all her failures, her vulnerabilities, and her shortcomings. He knows all of that stuff. He knows her history. He knows her better than she knows herself, and yet He still initiates the conversation and relationship. Most humans avoid people who they know to be broken, dysfunctional, abnormal, and defective. But Jesus doesn't.

Today, Jesus has initiated that relationship with you because He loves you. And He knows you better than you know yourself. He knows your failures. He knows those dark spots. He knows those weaknesses. He knows those vulnerabilities and dysfunctions. He knows where you have repeatedly had disaster and failure and hardship and struggle. He knows the relational struggles you've had and the failures you've had. He knows all of those. And yet today, He's still speaking to you and wants to have a conversation with you, but not just kind of go through the surface and the shallow, frothy stuff. He wants to zero down into that very raw, exposed nerve, that weakest vulnerability, where you are most defective—He wants to speak into that.

Number one, Jesus wants to expose that brokenness to uncover it and have a genuine, healthy, and constructive relationship with you. The deepest relationships have to have truth. You can't have intimacy without truth. Jesus wants that intimacy with you. So He goes and exposes that weak spot so that He can have a deeper relationship with you than ever before, to heal you and make you whole. This is exactly what He did with this Samaritan woman when He says, "Go and call your husband." And she says, "Hm, ah, (coughs) I have no husband." Jesus speaks straight to her issue and says in John 4:17-18, "Yep, that's accurate. You've had five husbands and the guy you're with now isn't your husband." Don't you know she was choking on her teeth!? What do you say to that? He just read all of her mail, took the deepest hurts in her life and in this brief discussion, put her deepest pain on the table for discussion - with a virtual stranger.

Take a step back and consider why she was there by herself? Think about it. Here's a woman who in her own town has had five husbands. She's sleeping with the sixth guy. She's had broken relationship after broken relationship, failed intimacy after failed intimacy. No wonder she's there by herself around noontime to draw water. She's probably been shamed and ostracized in her town. Perhaps the women in her town treated her with disdain and disgrace. Sometimes women can be catty with each other particularly when it comes to our relationships and vulnerabilities. We can be ruthless, take shots and jabs at each other and cut and hurt and say mean, cruel things. Well, no wonder she was there by herself. She probably wanted to avoid that entire social struggle and all those conflicts and all those mean things; but Jesus exposes the whole thing.

He blows it up on her and says, here's the real deal. You've had failure after failure after failure and I'm still having this conversation with you. I'm still here talking to you because I'm after your heart. I'm after a relationship with you.

Have you had broken relationships? Is your relationship with Jesus broken? Jesus wants to help you, but more than that, Jesus wants to heal you and restore your intimacy with Him. Jesus wants to take your pain, guilt, failure, discouragement, hopelessness, and brokenness and turn all of the mess into something beautiful. Pain in Jesus' hands can become perfume. Jesus wants to have an ongoing conversation with you and get to the nerve of what those issues and areas are. That's exactly what He did with this woman. He said, "Yeah, you've had five husbands. And the guy you're with now, he's not even your husband."

And so her response back, after she swallowed her teeth, was to change the subject—a classic ploy we use when we don't know what to say. "Let's change the subject and talk about something religious, since you're a Jewish man and it's well known that there's lots of religious conflict between Jews and Samaritans. Sir, I perceive that you're a prophet. Where is the proper place to worship?" Jesus continues this conversation and keeps talking with her about worship and worshipping God with the right heart. But He also does something breathtaking. As he keeps talking with this very broken woman, she brings up the whole topic of how when the Messiah comes, He will declare all things, make everything clear. And what Jesus says next is the most revolutionary thing He did throughout this entire exchange. The next thing that Jesus says in John 4:26 is, "'I who speak with you am He.'" We have to realize that Jesus not only revealed this woman's darkest secret, but with this simple statement, He also reveals to this broken, dysfunctional, and outcast Samaritan woman His most hidden identity up to that point. There's a good chance this Samaritan woman is the first person that Jesus lets know that He is the Messiah - maybe even before His disciples knew who He really was.

Perhaps it's true that the more we let Jesus know us the more we will get to know Jesus.

At this point, Jesus' disciples return from getting lunch in the city and they see Jesus talking with this Samaritan woman. They were amazed that Jesus had crossed over what was considered politically correct behavior and was talking with her. "What are you doing talking to a Samaritan woman?" they thought. Once the disciples show up, the Samaritan woman leaves her water jug there and she goes back to the town and this is what happened. In John 4:26-28, it says, "She went to the men in her town," the men, not just the women but to the men. I point this out to remind you that she had been a wife to five of those men and, and she probably had a reputation among them. She says to them, "Come and see a man who told me everything I ever did." Don't you know that the men in the town are like, "Whoa, we need to go and see who she's talking about." Maybe some of them were kind of nervous and maybe some of them were curious. Whatever their thinking, in John 4:30, it says that they went out of the city and were coming to Jesus. The results of this woman's announcement is very interesting, particularly in light of Jesus' disciples reaction when they brought Him lunch.

If you think about it, Jesus' disciples bring Him lunch because He was hungry and tired, which is totally great. Jesus needed that physical sustenance. In contrast, this woman doesn't bring Jesus lunch. She brings to Jesus her whole town. And that is often what happens when we have these kinds of conversations with Jesus and we are honest, vulnerable, and transparent with Him. When we say, "Look, I'm struggling. I'm having a hard time here. I've had these failures and I need Your help. I need You to bring truth into my life. Show me who You made me to be. Show me where I believed deception. Show me where I've been broken because of things that have happened in the past. Strengthen those weak spots. Deal with me and quickly, Holy Spirit come in. Give me strength. Be truth in my heart."

When we have those conversations with Jesus, then He redeems us. He repairs us. He restores us. He heals us so that we can go back and be a sign and a wonder because that's exactly what this woman did. And when she did that, the whole town came out. They're all like, "Wow, we need to go see who this guy really is. Oh, my goodness, here's the woman who has been kind of the town floozy and now she's talking openly with all of us about a very curious man. She's been redeemed, repaired, healed, and restored. We have to see this with our own eyes." And that's exactly what happened. The whole town comes out and to see Jesus. Jesus starts to talk with them - all because a broken, defective, and dysfunctional woman entered into a transformational conversation with Jesus.

When we have a genuine touch from Jesus, we're changed. We're never the same. We're transformed. He comes in and takes that brokenness, restores, redeems, repairs, and brings us back to wholeness. And the truth of it is, we cannot have wholeness in our relationships without first having that with Jesus. In the Samaritan woman's conversation with Jesus, he repaired, restored, and redeemed her so that she could go back and start to have healthy interactions in her town. And what her heart so deeply longed for was found by accident with Jesus when she was trying to isolate and withdraw. Jesus came smack into the middle of her dysfunction and initiated a transforming conversation. Jesus initiated the relationship out of genuine love. Jesus started a connection with her and her life was never the same.

After her revolutionary conversation with Jesus, her town came out to hear what this amazing man had to say. They listened to Jesus and this is what they said to her. After they listened to Jesus, they said, "You know, we were amazed by what you told us because there was clearly something really, really revolutionary about this guy, Jesus, whoever He is. But now that we've heard Him for ourselves, we believe." In John 4:43, it says that Jesus stayed there a couple days and the whole town basically came to Christ and put their faith and confidence in Jesus - all because of one broken woman who had failure after failure after failure, came to Jesus.

Jesus can do the same for you today. Jesus can heal you and redeem your relationships.

Consider a few of the following helpful action points:

- What's the honesty quotient in your relationship with Jesus?
- In what ways could Jesus heal you so that you could have more healthy relationships?
- Consider some people that you may need to forgive, including yourself.

MODERNEXAMPLE

Please remember that this section isn't designed to show you a perfect person but rather an inspiring woman who had some amazing moments and achievements. As you read about her, consider how God could work in your life to help you be a Jesus Chick.

IRENA SENDLER

Whenever we look· at someone's life, we can find great courage, admirable traits, and inspiring achievements. On the flip side, everyone is human with flaws, shortcomings, deficiencies, negative characteristics, and foibles. The ladies that I've chose to accentuate in each modern example section are every bit as human as you and me so if you dig around enough, you're sure to find they weren't perfect. My goal in this section is to inspire, encourage, and motivate us to see a possible modern counterpart or possible parallel to the Jesus Chicks in each chapter. Some of our Jesus Chicks are easy to make connections to in our modern living and some are a little more challenging. Nevertheless, please read about each as an encouraging example who might motivate each of us to be a Jesus Chick in our own unique way.

Irena Sendler was a polish social worker during WWII. She worked covertly to smuggle babies and children out of the Warsaw ghetto and saved the lives of approximately 2,500 Jewish babies and children from the atrocities of concentration camps during the Holocaust. While Irena was secretly smuggling out these babies and children (sometimes she would hide a baby in a toolbox), her efforts were discovered by the Nazis and she was tortured and sentenced to death for her covert defiance. She managed to survive the execution sentence, but after the Nazi's discovered her illegal activity, they brutally beat her and broke her legs.

After WWII, there were extensive efforts made to reunite these children with their parents, but unfortunately the majority of these parents' were killed in concentration camps or various other ways during the Holocaust. Nevertheless, Irena Sendler was a tremendous hero that has been memorialized in the twenty-first century for her life-saving work.

It's noteworthy to consider that possibly some of her motivation to put herself in such risky work came partly from her dad. When Irena was seven years old, her father, who was doctor, contracted typhus from treating patients whom other doctors refused to treat, many of whom were Jews.

I commemorate Mrs. Sendler in this chapter with the Samaritan woman because she put herself at great risk to save babies and make a difference in their future. Similarly, our Samaritan woman took a great risk after her conversation to bring the good news about Jesus back to her town. Because she took this risk, her whole town came to meet Jesus and be transformed by His message.

CHAPTER 2
OPULENT LOVE
Being Defended by Jesus
Mary of Bethany

Have you ever had someone come to your defense when you were doing something possibly controversial yet you knew to your very core was the right thing to do? Recently one of my friends came under attack in their workplace and was being unfairly accused of something that was wrong. I immediately wanted to jump in and rescue my friend, but I also knew that I needed to be wise and strategic about my actions and words. For a while there was lots of anxiety and stress because of the unfair accusation, but in the end, my friend was vindicated because she was right and the accusations were wrong.

This type of challenge isn't unusual, but it can be really painful - particularly when the accusation comes from a family member. This is exactly what happened with Martha and Mary of Bethany when we are introduced to these sisters in Luke 10:38-42. I love who Mary of Bethany was, particularly in this story. Mary of Bethany was a sister to Martha. And when you think about Mary of Bethany, she's one of the coolest Jesus Chicks. I love her because she's a very real human and an easy person to whom we can relate. In Luke 10 Jesus is making a journey to Jerusalem and on His way, He passes through Bethany. While Jesus is in Bethany, He accepted an invitation for dinner at the house of Martha and Mary, which is what we read about in verses 38-42. In this first visit with Martha and Mary, we briefly read that Mary was sitting at Jesus' feet listening to Him teach and Martha was doing all of the dinner preparation. In a very typical sisterly conflict, Martha asks Jesus to make Mary help her with dinner. The way that Martha makes this request to Jesus seems kind of harsh and accusative.

In the background of these verses, you can see that both sisters have two very different personalities, mindsets, and priorities. Martha is playing the consummate hostess role and Mary seems to be the "lazy one", not carrying her fair share of the workload. Martha was really concerned about all of the work she had to do and about hosting their guests well. After all, Jesus was a very important man - lots of miracles, amazing teaching, religious leaders around him, and generally very influential. Martha is what I would call the "hostess with the mostest": let's be sure that the floor is clean, the kitchen is organized, maybe she was concerned about the laundry and much more because she was having Jesus at her house. If you were in Martha's shoes, you might have the same reaction – "let's get this place straightened up, Jesus is coming for dinner!"

When we have important people for dinner at our house and we're trying to impress them, we go to GREAT lengths to hide the counter clutter (scoop it all in a box and throw the box in the closet), make a really delicious meal, coach the kids ahead of time about proper conversational etiquette (don't talk about what hotdogs are really made of), general cleaning, straightening up and we try to make our home look less "lived in" and more "Martha Stewart-ish" despite having a very active and busy family with three kids involved in everything from drums to football to geography club to volleyball. This was Martha. She wants to honor Jesus. And I think she has a right heart. She wants to make Jesus feel like an esteemed guest, that He's special and important. And she went to these lengths to make Him feel welcome - maybe she was also insecure.

Mary, on the flip side, is not like that. She's more laid back, easy going and into connecting with Jesus. Her priority is to hang out and be with Jesus. It didn't seem to bother her if there was laundry, dirty dishes, counter clutter, a messy kitchen, or a pristine presentation. Jesus Christ was in her house and that's what was important to Mary. When you think about it, Martha and Mary represent two different mindsets, of which neither of them is necessarily wrong. Martha wants to honor Jesus. Mary wants to be with Jesus. But in many respects, Mary is more relational than Martha in these verses. Consequently, Mary winds up sitting at Jesus' feet and that's a really important thing for us to consider.

Now I'm going to walk you through what that means historically because there's some significance on what Mary decided to do. At this time in history during Jesus' life, the cultural norms and social expectations were that the women were supposed to hang out in the kitchen, cook everything, do the cleaning, and stay in all of the roles that were proper for women at this time. A woman could possibly hang out at the meal, but women certainly didn't have a lot of interaction with the men. There were very traditional male roles and traditional female roles, especially at this time. And so, for Mary to come and hang out and sit at Jesus' feet, or any man's feet in Israel, was a big problem.

Historically, the people who sat at another person's feet were people who were learners. Sitting at the feet was the pose of a student with a teacher. So when Mary came and made the decision to sit at Jesus' feet, she positioned herself as a learner. Now, understand that at this time, it wasn't very common for women to be educated and certainly not in the law or religious things. The women were educated in things like the kitchen, kids, cleaning, cooking, laundry, and all things domestic. Women weren't expected to learn from religious leaders in legal, religious, or spiritual issues. Those topics weren't appropriate for women to learn about. So when Mary sat at Jesus' feet it wasn't just necessarily a personality conflict between Martha with the domestic minded stuff.

From our modern point of view, it seems like Mary was more chilled out and relaxed than her sister Martha. But when we dig into the history and culture, there's more to it than just two different mindsets. When Mary sat at Jesus' feet, understand that she positioned herself with other men who were sitting at Jesus' feet to learn from him. Mary stepped out of the cultural norm, what was common, comfortable, and accepted, to do something exceptional. And when she did that, Martha kind of slapped her down. I think there was more to Martha's complaint than just getting Mary to help with the workload. I think there was also somewhere in Martha's thinking, "This is not acceptable. Mary, you're defying the cultural norms and you need to stop doing that and start helping me. Come on Jesus, make Mary conform to the social norms and what is culturally acceptable."

If you think about it, Mary wanted to learn from Jesus at the tremendous risk of rejecting social norms and upsetting her family relationships. And let's never forget that when you come after Jesus, He says, "Seek and ye shall find. Knock and it will be open to you. Ask and you will receive" (Matt 7:7). And this is exactly what Mary was doing. She was saying, "Jesus, I want to learn from you - I want a relationship with you, I want to sit at your feet and hear what you've got to say. I want to be in your presence more than I want to clean the dishes." Mary didn't seem to care if her behavior violated the cultural norms or even made her sister upset with her. She wanted to be close to Jesus, sitting at his feet and defying what's culturally acceptable. Being with Jesus was important to Mary.

I think that Jesus' reply to Martha is extremely enlightening and gives us a powerful insight into Jesus' priorities. Jesus doesn't say, "Oh, my goodness, Mary. Who do you think you are? You're a woman. You shouldn't be doing this. This is completely wrong. High tail it back to the kitchen so you can stay where you're supposed to be with your sister, Martha." Instead of staying in the groove with what we'd call politically correct, Jesus validates Mary's quest, journey, and desire to be with Him. Jesus said to Martha, "You know Martha, Mary has made the right choice. And what she's decided will not be taken from her."

When you make a decision to pursue Jesus, not just His hand and what He can do for you, but a decision to pursue Him for His face, for who He is, Jesus will validate that decision and pursuit saying, "Yep, you made the right choice. You made the right choice to come after Me." Even if it wasn't popular with your family. Even if you went against the grain in your culture and society. Even if the social norms say, "Blah, that's kind of weird and crazy. You shouldn't be going to those extremes." Jesus will say, "Yeah, if you come after Me, you're going to find Me. If you ask for Me, I'm going to reveal Myself to you. If you knock, I'm going to open the door."

When we pursue Jesus, His answer to us is always "Yes!! I want that relationship and I want that connection with you!" And when you begin the adventure of a personal relationship with Jesus, He changes the game. Everything changes because of who Jesus is. And we can see this change play out in the relationship Martha and Mary had with Jesus. This became a really cool relationship. And the meal at Martha and Mary's house was the ground zero formation of that relationship.

Being Disappointed with Jesus

So let's consider the next place we see Martha and Mary interact with Jesus and this is in John 11. Up to this point, Martha and Mary had developed a nice friendship with Jesus and established a nice connection, which is evidenced by how Martha and Mary addressed Jesus in John 11. In this chapter, Lazarus, their brother, is really sick. So they call for Jesus who is off in some other town or village a long distance from Bethany, their hometown. They send for Jesus and let him know that their brother, Lazarus, is really sick and they need Him to come and heal him." We know that a really nice relationship had developed between Jesus, Martha, Mary, and Lazarus because when the sisters sent for Jesus, they said in John 11:3, "Lord, behold, the one *whom you love* is sick." In verse 5 it adds that Jesus loved Martha and Mary. Nevertheless, despite their request Jesus did something really weird. In John 11:6 it says that Jesus stayed two more days where He was and didn't come immediately when He was summoned. Jesus waited until Lazarus died before He set out. And when He finally came to Bethany, Martha heard that Jesus was coming.

As a quick refresher, remember, Martha had been very concerned about her domestic responsibilities when she first had Jesus over for dinner. But now, with her brother being dead, it was the cultural norm to have lots of people come to your home when there was a death to help and be a support with all of the grief and mourning from the loss of a loved one. Nevertheless, Martha leaves the house to come and be with Jesus and they have an interesting conversation about how Jesus is the resurrection and the life. Martha gets an inside revelation of who Jesus is and we'll talk more about this in our chapter on Martha.

But for now, we are focusing on Mary and here's the irony in this story. When we first met Mary, she defied the social norms to be with Jesus. But in this situation, Mary stays back at the house. Possibly she was frustrated and upset with Jesus. When she finally does come to Jesus, her first words were pretty accusative, "Had you been here, our brother would not have died."

Have you ever been frustrated and upset with Jesus? It's an important question. I think all of us have been frustrated with Jesus from time to time. Perhaps Jesus didn't do what you wanted Him to do. Maybe you prayed to Jesus and it seemed like He didn't answer. Maybe Jesus' timing is out of sync with your plans and schedule. Similar to disappointments and frustrations we sometimes have with Jesus, Mary was also hurt and disappointed with Jesus. Maybe she was thinking, "Look, buddy, we sent for You. We know You can do that healing the sick thing. We gave You time to come and make a difference and keep Lazarus from dying. And You didn't come. For whatever reason You stayed away and now he's dead. And now, I'm extremely disappointed in You - You let me down and I'm frustrated, angry, upset, bitter, and mad because You didn't do what you're supposed to do. You're the healer and now he's dead and it's too late. It's all over."

When we first met Mary in Luke 10, she was the one that was all engaged, connected, and hanging out with Jesus, maybe breathless for every word that came out of His mouth. But now she's hurt. She's disappointed. And so she pulls back and withdraws. Sometimes we do the same thing with Jesus. I was talking with a friend of mine the other day and as we were talking and she said to me, "I'm really mad at God. I don't like these things that I've seen and I've read in the newspaper about some atrocities in our nation and around the world. I'm really upset. How can a good God who is all powerful allow such horrible things to happen? I'm mad at God." She thought I was going to get upset, but I didn't. Instead, I replied, "I think that's good and I don't think it's necessarily bad or wrong to be mad at God, at various times in our lives. I think it's good to wrestle with God and talk to Him, letting God know your frustrations. On occasion, I've said to God, "I'm frustrated with you. I think you did the wrong thing and I don't like your answer. It makes me angry and upset."

In my way of thinking, it's better to have some honest conflict and wrestle than to pull away and make distance the result of your disappointment. Don't separate yourself like Mary did when her brother died. Come to Jesus and be honest with Him. Take the approach, "I'm hurt and I don't like the outcome, but I'm not leaving you." Some people decide to take a break from Jesus and move on when they don't get their requests answered the way that they want. Don't be that person. Other people I've known bring their frustration, disappointments, questions, and pain to Jesus, remaining connected despite their feelings.

That's the difference between Martha and Mary in John 11. Martha is definitely upset. Mary is also very upset and her behavior says, "I'm going to keep my distance from Jesus. I'm going to stay at home and I'm going to withdraw and I'm going to isolate." Have you ever stopped going to church because you're mad at someone who hurt you? Sometimes when we stop going to church we also distance ourselves from Jesus. If anything, withdrawing from Jesus makes it worse because the truth of it is, we need Jesus. We need Jesus in our brokenness; we need Jesus in our bitterness. We need Jesus in our disappointment. We need Jesus because we're not going to come out of any of that stuff better, and not bitter or broken, without Him. We desperately need Jesus. You need Him in your life and you need Him smack in the middle of all that stuff because that is how we're designed: to need Jesus. Regardless of whether you're having tremendous success or abysmal failure, we need Jesus.

Despite Mary's withdrawal, Martha goes back to her after her chat with Jesus and says, "Hey, guess what, Jesus is asking for you." And so Mary gets up, goes out and she falls at Jesus' feet. I think this is really powerful about Mary because the first time we met her, she was learning at Jesus' feet. And now she's weeping at Jesus' feet - hurt, angry and disappointed. In a really healthy way, she's bringing Him all of her emotional frustration. Mary falls at Jesus' feet and says, "Lord, if you'd been here, my brother wouldn't have died." And this is completely true. By nature, Jesus heals. When you read about Jesus in the Gospels, virtually everywhere He goes people get healed because that's who He is. Healing is natural for Jesus. But here's the completely astounding thing in this whole story:

Jesus had something better in mind than just healing. Jesus had resurrection on His mind. Jesus knew what He was going to do. He knew that Lazarus was going to die. He knew that Martha and Mary would be upset with Him. He knew He'd see all the Jews mourning and upset. He knew all this stuff. And He still let Lazarus die because He had a "bigger" miracle in mind than what Martha and Mary had requested. They asked Jesus to come and heal their brother. I don't really think that they had resurrection on their mind. Maybe Martha had an inkling of this idea after her chat with Jesus, but not Mary.

Don't be like Mary and hold on to your frustration, bitterness, disappointment, and hurt. Don't hold on to that more than you hold on to Jesus. Sometimes we make that mistake and holding on to the hurt, pain, anger, unforgiveness and more, but that stuff never helps us. But holding on to Jesus always redeems, restores, and repairs us. There is resurrection when we hold onto Jesus.

When Jesus sees Mary and the Jews weeping, this is the only place in the Bible, besides Gethsemane, where we see that Jesus wept. Jesus wept because He saw the grief, mourning, and disappointment. He felt their pain. He felt their emotions and grieving. He felt all of that.

But He gets moving and says, "Show me, where's Lazarus?" So they take Him to the tomb and Jesus says, "Roll back the stone." Shortly thereafter, Jesus said, "Lazarus come forth" and here comes Lazarus in the grave clothes, hopping out of the tomb. He's risen from the dead. I love Jesus because He's the ultimate game changer. There was sickness and now we know He can heal. There was death and now we know He can raise from the dead. He changes the whole dynamic. I mean, He's the ultimate, epic game changer. You have to expect the unexpected with Jesus. And that's exactly what happened. Martha and Mary, I think they were like, "Oh, uh". What do you say to that? They are totally blown away - they had healing in mind, but Jesus trumped that with resurrection!

Let's take one more look at Mary before we finish this chapter because the next time we see her, in John 12, it's a really powerful display of her love for Jesus. When we first meet Mary, she is a learner, sitting at Jesus' feet. The next time we connect with her, she's a weeper, disappointed and hurt. And in our relationship with Jesus, there's a good possibility from time to time that we can also get disappointed. We do get hurt and Mary models for us what we should and shouldn't do. We should not isolate or withdraw. We shouldn't pull back from Jesus because we need Him. Let's fall at His feet and bring our emotions to Him. Bring the hardships, the disappointments, frustrations, anger, hurt, and all of those things that are so very painful. Bring all of that to Jesus. It doesn't overwhelm Him nor stress Him out. The truth of it is, Jesus is the place where all those things can be healed, restored, and repaired. Jesus can bring resurrection. Nothing's impossible with Jesus.

But now in John, chapter 12, we see Martha and Mary again and I love this one. This is just breathtaking. Mary in her progression started as a learner, then bringing Him her emotions, as a weeper. Now in John 12, we see Mary as one who is deeply in love with Jesus and demonstrates this by pouring out her love for him. In this chapter, we read that she weeps over His feet, washes His feet with her tears, dries His feet with her hair, anoints Him, and kisses His feet because she's now come through this progression. As a result, she has a deep, heartfelt relationship with Jesus that she never had before. Don't you know when she was sitting at His feet learning she was getting a glimpse, a taste of who Jesus is and the richness and the magnificent fellowship, the intimacy, the depth of relationship she could have with Him? She went through that dark hard time, and now she's come out on the other side and she has one of the deepest, richest, most vibrant, most committed, connected relationships with Jesus of any woman in the Bible - all through a progression, in which she didn't quit and give up.

Hopefully as you read this today, you are also challenged to have a similar depth of relationship with Jesus through your distinct journey, learning, weeping, and loving. I'm telling you, Jesus loves you today and wants to have that deep relationship with you.

Consider a few of the following action points that could be helpful.

- What are the painful areas in your life that you might be withholding from Jesus?

- Has something happened in the past that you've allowed to put distance between you and Jesus?

- Pray for someone you know that is going through a rough time - pray that they will come to know Jesus better than they ever did before through this hardship.

31

MODERNEXAMPLE

Please remember that this section isn't designed to show you a perfect person but rather an inspiring woman who had some amazing moments and achievements. As you read about her, consider how God could work in your life to help you be a Jesus Chick.

MALLORY JOHNSON

When I was thinking about a modern woman who would be an example of Mary of Bethany, I started looking into various women but I was struggling to find someone like Mary. In my way of looking at Mary, she was very devoted, abandoned with her love, and uncommonly relational. When I looked for someone famous with these characteristics, I had a difficult time finding a "fit." I started thinking about some of the women with whom I'm friends and I found the perfect person. Because my friend is very alive today, I'm changing her name to protect the innocent, so to speak. We'll call my friend Mallory Johnson.

Mallory is the mom of several kids, she's happily married and she is totally amazing. I love her for many of reasons, but maybe one very strong reason why I love her is because she is so overflowing with her love—ebullient is the best word I could find to describe how she loves. Mallory's love for people doesn't have pre-conditions, strings, expectations, or qualifications and the only people she makes feel jittery are the religious folk with puckered lips, lemony balm, and prickly words. She hasn't come from a heavy duty religious family nor does she have extravagant wealth, but she's deep in the weeds with loving people in daily ways; heartfelt connections, and genuine presence. I could totally see my friend Mallory sitting at Jesus' feet, soaking in His teaching. I could see my friend being upset with Jesus in dealing with the loss of a loved one and the most comfortable thing I could see my friend doing is washing Jesus' feet with her tears, anointing Him and kissing His feet. My friend Mallory loves with ebullient love.

CHAPTER 3
HOPELESSNESS
Woman with the Issue of Blood

I had a friend who was doing well in her career and relatively healthy, but had a few weak spots in her relationships and some of her thinking. Unfortunately, these weak spots began to grow and over the course of time, her thinking became very dark. My husband and I talked with her regularly and really tried to encourage her, but she got stuck in her thinking and seemed unable to get out of the quagmire of darkness and she became hopeless. Over time, the darkness consumed her and she tragically took her life. My husband and I were of course stunned at her decision and when I think about her life today, I still feel pain from her decision and saddness for her family. At the end of her life, she couldn't see any other way to deal with her pain and despair. Being hopeless is a dangerous place for our thinking - dangerous to us and to the people in our lives.

But I know there is always hope even in the darkest times of our lives. There's a story in Mark 5 that totally speaks to the eternal presence of hope and this story is about a woman who seemed to be in a totally impossible situation. In this chapter, we read about a woman who had a physical infirmity and she was totally despondent. She had an issue of blood – meaning she was bleeding in a female way and was unable to stop this bleeding for twelve continuous years. Of course this became a tremendous problem for her in many different ways. First of all, in Jesus' day, they obviously didn't have access to the medical facilities and knowledge that we have today. She was bleeding from her body for twelve consecutive years. That's a long time-that's a very, very long time. In Mark 5, it says that she continued to get worse and worse. She went to doctors. She spent all the money she had on doctors and nothing helped, she only continued to deteriorate.

Medical problems:
When you think about this, a person who has continuous bleeding for twelve years has an extremely depleted and trashed body. Her body is severely iron deficient. She had many physical complications from this condition. From her perspective, she was in a very hopeless situation. But she must have had just enough strength and a sliver of hope left because she took a chance and came out in public to connect with Jesus.

Social problems:
To get some cultural and historical perspective, it's important for us to understand that it was forbidden by the religious law (by Moses in Leviticus and Deuteronomy) for this woman to be in public because of her continuous bleeding. With her condition, if she had been discovered in public, she was at risk of being stoned (killed) for breaking this religious law. So this woman is taking a great personal chance to make this connection with Jesus and perhaps in her thinking, Jesus is her last and only hope. I like her thinking because she didn't totally give up hope. Her behavior is a cool model – no situation with Jesus is

hopeless. So she took a risk going out and pressing through a very dense crowd. And the crowd was dense because everyone wanted to connect with Jesus. Jesus' reputation preceded Him and created quite a stir.

Despite being controversial, Jesus was cool back then and He's still totally cool today. If you and I could get around Jesus and nudge up next to him in a crowd, I'd want to be the first one to press in. Any opportunity to hang out with Jesus is beyond golden! I'd want to grab His elbow and see if we could take a little walk with a nice chat. In my experience, genuine Jesus is wholly irresistible and thoroughly magnetic. So here is our friend, the woman who is desperate, making possibly her last and final attempt to get better, pushing her way through a big crowd and trying to go unnoticed, potentially risking her life. She was in such a desperate situation that she took extreme measures to try and get help and healing. The Bible says in Mark 5:28, she thought, "If I just touch his clothes, I will be healed." (NIV) Her desperation caused her to take drastic measures – risking her very life just to touch a piece of Jesus' clothing. In the meantime, Jesus was on a mission to go with a Jewish leader of the law named Jairus to heal his 12-year-old daughter when this very sick and desperate woman takes this life-threatening chance.

In my heart, I believe that you and I desperately need Jesus throughout all of the aspects of our lives. For myself, I need Jesus so I can be a good wife and I need Jesus so I can be a good mom. Furthermore, I need Jesus so I can be a good daughter and fundamentally, I need Jesus so I can be a good human. We need Jesus in our thinking because sometimes our thoughts are really wacky and even yucky. We can get pretty messed up in our thoughts but Jesus can straighten out our thinking. We need Jesus in our emotions and feelings because if we're not careful, our feelings can try to be stronger than our faith. But Jesus helps not only our thinking but also our emotions and feelings. We need Jesus in our relationships because sometimes we have unhealthy relationships. We need Jesus to be involved in our relationships and to repair them so they can be healthy and constructive. We need Jesus to touch our physical bodies where we have maladies and sicknesses and illnesses and weaknesses. We desperately need Jesus. And my sense is that Jesus is the answer for our lives regardless if everything is going super smooth or if things are really rough and rocky. I believe that Jesus is the answer for our lives more than our best talent or ability, more than our highest intelligence, more than our most beautiful physique or attire or anything that could possibly be "the best" in our lives. Jesus is the answer in the very core of who we are and for our decisions and the purpose for our lives.

For the woman with the issue of blood, she also came to the conclusion that she needed Jesus more than anything else in her life. She had no other hope, no other solutions, and no other alternatives. One of the things I love about this woman is she acknowledges her need for Jesus and she doesn't try and cover it up and do all this smoke screen stuff. She doesn't try to get all religious and pious or self-justifying. Her behavior simply reveals the truth that she knew in her heart – that she needed Jesus and that was her ground zero. Another important observation about this woman is that when she presses through the crowd to touch Jesus' clothing, she presses through with faith and not doubt or pessimism. She's at a place in her life where she has nothing left but faith and desperation. Her behavior doesn't reveal ambivalence, indifference or a "let's try and see if this works" attitude. Her actions reflected her faith and we know from James 2:17 that faith without works is dead.

Because of her faith in action, right when she touched the hem of Jesus' garment, the Bible says that she could perceive in her body that she was well. Can you imagine what that felt like? Put yourself in her sandals. Maybe she felt some kind of charge or a rush in her body, some kind of healing and transforming touch. But whatever she felt, she knew that for the first time in twelve years something was altogether different. There's a dramatic change and everything was no longer the same after she touched Jesus' garment.

But here is where the entire situation changes because Jesus became aware of power leaving Him. Jesus perceived that something very dramatic and powerful had happened and that power had gone out of Him. He immediately stops his journey to Jairus' house. He stops in the middle of this crowd and puts everything on hold to figure out what just happened because whatever just happened was more significant than continuing His journey at that moment. In Luke 8:45-46, Jesus says, "Someone touched me because I can tell that power has gone out of Me." Jesus turns to His disciples and asks them, "Who touched me?" I love what His disciples say to Him. Basically, they respond to Him and say, "Seriously? You're surrounded by hundreds of people and they're all pressing in and jostling you and touching you. The more appropriate question would be, 'Who didn't touch Me?' How on earth are we supposed to figure out who touched You?!?" That's like trying to find a needle in a haystack. But Jesus doesn't let it slide. He continues to press on with His question, "Who touched Me? Something happened here and power went out from Me. I have to find out what happened."

Now here's something for your consideration. Jesus already knew who touched Him because He knows everything. He already knew what happened with this woman who had an issue of blood and who pushed through the crowd to touch His garment. Jesus already knew that power had gone out from Him and He knew that the woman was healed. Furthermore, Jesus knew who she was but He stops the whole crowd and the whole journey. And here's what I would suggest to you: He stops the whole journey to single out this woman with the issue of blood. And remember that under Jewish Law it was illegal for this woman to be out in public because she's unclean and was violating Jewish law. But Jesus singles her out and He does this because she is now clean, and she can be in public without the fear of being stoned or ostracized. Now she doesn't have to live under the shame or the guilt or the uncleanness or the weakness or the infirmity. She doesn't have to live under that. Now she can come out in public and not be afraid of being killed and not have to sneak places or hide or withdraw because of the uncleanness.

She can safely be in public and have a "normal" life because she was made well and whole from the top of her head down to her toes with no more shame, no more uncleanness, no more infirmity, no more sickness-after twelve years of hardship, desperation and weakness. All of this was removed with one touch of Jesus' garment. And this is what happens when we connect with Christ. He changes us and all of the shame and guilt goes away because of what Jesus does and Who Jesus is.

So after she touches His garment, she is never the same and Jesus calls her out to make her miracle public. He doesn't let her slink off and keep a secret miracle. Jesus exposes her miracle perhaps so that she can come out in public without being afraid of being unclean or being stoned or being a social outcast or ostracized. Jesus' miracle isn't only for her body but consider that Jesus' miracles often have a ripple effect into other areas of our lives as well. Jesus' miracle for this hopeless woman heals her body and now He makes it very publically visible that this woman has been made well socially not just physically. Her body was made well along with her position in society and even her personal relationships by the power of Jesus. And this is one of the things that I so deeply love about Jesus—His touch works its way into every single facet of our lives if we give Him the chance...if we say yes.

And with beautiful faith, the woman pressed through the crowd for a physical healing but Jesus didn't settle for only that miracle. By calling her out and drawing attention to her, He multiplied the miracle so that her one touch of faith carried over into many of different areas in her life. After twelve years of infirmity and weakness, twelve years of being a social outcast and being afraid of getting stoned, Jesus restores, redeems, and repairs her far beyond her initial focus.

But here's the double whammy for hopelessness. Before we read about this woman who has been bleeding for twelve continuous years, we understand that Jairus had come up to Jesus in the middle of a really big crowd and asks Jesus to come with him to heal his twelve-year-old daughter who is at death's door. He explains that his daughter is about to die and that he wants Jesus to come and heal her and raise her up. In this one story, there are two women in totally hopeless situations and both coming to Jesus in their unique ways. But ultimately, Jesus is the cure for anything that is hopeless. He is the author, origin, and embodiment of authentic hope and with Jesus, no situation, hardship, difficulty, illness, relationship, job, concern, or worry is hopeless. After He hears what Jairus says about his daughter, Jesus agrees to go with Jairus to heal her and this is where the woman with the issue of blood pops up on the scene-in the middle of Jesus' journey to heal Jairus' daughter. As Jesus is journeying to Jairus' house to heal his little girl, He pauses for a few minutes to deal with the woman with the issue of blood. After this brief pause, somebody comes up to Jairus and lets him know that it's too late, that his daughter has just died. But basically Jesus says that if Jairus will believe, his little girl will be healed.

I'd like to show you some interesting contrasts with these two women: the older woman with the issue of blood and the twelve-year-old daughter of Jairus. Both women were *hopeless*:

- The woman with the issue of blood is totally hopeless. She has been sick for twelve years and couldn't get better. The doctors didn't help—nothing worked.

- Jairus' daughter has died.

But here's something interesting to consider. While Jesus was on the way to heal Jairus' daughter, whose father was a leader in the Jewish law, a woman comes out and breaks the law to touch Jesus' garment and receive her miracle. Furthermore, the woman with the issue of blood was entirely by herself; in contrast, Jairus was the advocate for his daughter. He interceded with Jesus on behalf of his daughter. However, the woman with the issue of blood had no one to intercede for her, she was all alone. There's a little girl who's twelve years old who is now dead and there's an older woman who has been sick for twelve years. Both of these women, one young, one old, received a touch from Jesus.

Regardless of the report that Jairus heard, Jesus went with him to his house and encouraged Jairus not to quit, give up, or be hopeless. I'm so thankful that Jesus stays on the journey of life with us, even when we get bad news, when we get discouraged or even hopeless. Jesus doesn't quit or give up and He continually encourages us to be better believers than doubters. Truly, Jesus is the Author of hope and He makes all things new, including Jairus' daughter. We see this in the way He spoke to Jairus, his friends, and his daughter upon arriving at their house. Sometimes when we are in dark or seemingly hopeless seasons in our lives, we must decide to keep walking with Jesus because the reality is that Jesus makes all things better and can bring resurrection out of death. When Jesus arrived at Jairus' house, He spoke to his daughter and raised her from the dead. After raising Jairus' daughter from the dead, don't you know Jairus' jaw probably dropped to the floor in total shock?! He probably thought, "Oh my goodness! How did You do that?" It's highly likely that Jesus' miracle of raising Jairus' daughter to life probably spread throughout the family and into the synagogue and the community. Let's face it, walking with Jesus is truly one of the greatest adventures in our lives!

As we bring the story of these two women into our personal lives, we must see that no matter where we are in our lives and no matter if you're totally hopeless and you've done it all wrong with lots of failures and shortcomings, no matter what your situation is, Jesus is our hope. Jesus comes to you today and says that He wants to make you well and whole. Let's respond by pressing in with faith and belief, saying, "Yes Jesus, I believe and trust in You. Yes Jesus, I have confidence in You. Yes Jesus, I know that You can make me well from the inside all the way to the outside." Jesus repairs, redeems, and restores.

So when you look at the woman with the issue of blood, she's got big time issues. And when you look at Jairus' daughter, she's got big issues as well. Both women are hopeless and desperately need help. One woman is all alone and isolated and can't seem to get any improvement no matter what she tries. Jairus' daughter isn't alone because she has her dad advocating on her behalf with her family around to be supportive and helpful. But nevertheless, nothing is helping either of these women – they're both in the same hopeless situation. Both women need Jesus and the truth of it is, both you and I need Jesus in every area of our lives. We need Jesus in our relationships, our physical and emotional health, in our planning and for our future. Furthermore, we need Jesus in our families, our work places, schools, in all areas and at all times. Jesus is truly our Hope.

Consider a few of the following action points that could be helpful:

- What areas in your life would you consider to be hopeless and how can you bring them to Jesus?

- Think of a time in your life when something seemed hopeless and that same something was completely revolutionized.

- Do risks cause you to compromise your faith and settle for mediocre or average?

MODERNEXAMPLE

Please remember that this section isn't designed to show you a perfect person but rather an inspiring woman who had some amazing moments and achievements. As you read about her, consider how God could work in your life to help you be a Jesus Chick.

SISTER ROSEMARY NYIRUMBE

Let me briefly introduce you to Sister Rosemary Nyirumbe from Uganda in Africa. Sister Rosemary is a Catholic nun who has been working for more than thirty years with girls who are victims of Joseph Kony's "Lords Resistance Army", LRA. Sister Rosemary has been the Director of St. Monica's Girls' Tailoring Center since 2001 where more than 200 girls receive training, education, and the opportunity to be transformed by Jesus' love. The majority of the girls whom Sister Rosemary has helped were severely traumatized because of being kidnapped and abused by the LRA. Because of the hope and genuine love that Sister Rosemary and her team offer, more than 2,000 hopeless, broken, and shattered girls have been redeemed and restored through consistent love, steady training, and engaged transformation they receive at St. Monica's.

Perhaps Sister Rosemary is touching the hem of Jesus' garment on behalf of these thousands of broken girls to bring them hope, healing, and a healthy, vibrant future.

CHAPTER 4
GOOD DECISIONS
Martha

I'm really BUSY! This seems to be the mantra of today's modern woman and yet I can't help wondering if this adjective applies to a universal and timeless pocket of women who find their value and significance in their achievements and being busy. I say this because I've always been aware, in our church and from my travels, of various women who seem to always be on the verge of collapse, fatigue and burned out. They exude stress and always seem like they are one second away from exploding or imploding. For example, I have a friend who has spent the majority of her life in "achieve mode" and she can easily fall into the deception trap that says, "You aren't valuable, significant, or important if you're not busy and achieving." I get it. In the past, I used to write easy tasks on my to-do list for no other reason than the gratification I felt from crossing them off my list. It's a really common but dangerous trap in which many women find themselves destructively deep in quagmire.

Thankfully, there was a woman in Jesus' life who probably had some of these same challenges and this is Martha, the sister to both Mary of Bethany and Lazarus. The first time we get to meet Martha, she's in her normal "busy" mindset. It's comforting to know that there were women in Jesus' life who had these same types of challenges that we deal with today. Consider the first interaction that we read about with Martha in Luke 10:38-42

38 *Now as they were traveling along, He entered a village; and a woman named Martha welcomed Him into her home.*

39 *She had a sister called Mary, who was seated at the Lord's feet, listening to His word.*

40 *But Martha was distracted with all her preparations; and she came up to Him and said, "Lord, do You not care that my sister has left me to do all the serving alone? Then tell her to help me."*

41 *But the Lord answered and said to her, "Martha, Martha, you are worried and bothered about so many things;*

42 *but only one thing is necessary, for Mary has chosen the good part, which shall not be taken away from her."*

I think these verses are great because they show us Martha as a really universal and timeless woman. You could find a woman saying this type of thing at any given time in history and throughout almost any culture. Perhaps you are even kind of like Martha and often find yourself in

- the labor mode more than the listen mode

- the achieve mode more than the affection mode

- the work mode more than the welcome mode

While I don't think that it's inherently wrong to work, achieve or labor, but if these things don't foster a deeper relationship and connection with Jesus, then maybe we aren't doing them in the right way? I say this because I'm very sympathetic with Martha. I have three kids, I'm happily married and I have a very demanding and rigorous life that overflows with expectations, responsibilities, and activities. I could easily be a Martha type person and try to whip everyone into the same mindset of achieve, work, accomplish, do, labor, clean, cook, scour, organize, facilitate, and more and more and more and more - suffocating any relational connections in my life. When Martha asked Jesus to make Mary help her, she was basically asking that Mary be forced to stop listening, stop learning, stop connecting, and start working, laboring, achieving, and doing. "Please make Mary put any relational development with You on hold so that she can help me get some work done around this place!"

Which begs the question, why did they invite Jesus to their house in the first place? Did they invite him so that they could ignore him while they cooked, cleaned, and worked? Seriously? But here's our problem as busy women with lots of responsibilities: we can't just withdraw and stop working. We have families for whom we need to cook. Our kids play on sports teams and have extracurricular activities that require transportation. Our husbands need us to do laundry (or they do it for us and we get to do the folding). We have jobs that demand us to show up and contribute if we want to continue being paid. We have friendships we want to maintain that require some level of ownership and interaction. And don't even think of adding in any kind of exercise schedule or routine - that can move us into the red overload zone with a potential crash and burn! None of these things include any volunteer responsibilities that we may have undertaken at church, in our communities, or elsewhere. With all of this stuff, it's tempting to say, "Stop the world, I want off!" Let's give Martha some credit; at least she was being responsible and not "lazy" like her sister, Mary.

But when Martha brings her problem to Jesus, thinking that He will support her request, He goes off the rails and says what Martha least expects. Jesus validates and affirms Mary's decision to sit as His feet, learning from and connecting with Him. In fact, Jesus applauds Mary's decision and says that what Mary has chosen won't be taken from her.

So what does this look like in our modern living, with laundry, dishes, homework, responsibilities, etc? We can't ignore the laundry and offering our family cereal for 3 meals a day won't work for long. We can't move away to a convent and leave all of our responsibilities, blessings, and relationships. So what can we do? How do we manage a busy and demanding life and concurrently engage and deepen our relationship with Jesus? Martha's solution was to stop the learning and start the laboring - that's the only answer she could propose to her problem - but there's another way.

Consider this, instead of stopping the relationship development with Jesus so Mary could go get some work done, maybe they could have asked Jesus to help them with their work. I know that this idea probably sounds dishonoring and even disrespectful at first glance, but let's take a minute to think about this. Martha and Mary didn't invite Jesus into their home so that they could ignore Him and in a similar way, I don't want Jesus in my life as an occasional visitor that pops over on special occasions and with special invitations, like Christmas and Easter. But instead of stopping the relational development that was happening between Jesus and Mary, perhaps Martha could have asked Jesus to join their work, maybe even do one of His miracle things. Ok, that's a little cheeky, but let me role this out for you in more practical terms.

Let's get practical: While we live busy lives, it doesn't mean that we need to ostracize or sideline our relationship with Jesus but rather let's integrate Jesus into our daily living. For example, one time I was having a really cool lunch with a friend and we were talking about our morning prayer times with Jesus. We were both expressing how wonderful it is to read the Bible and sit quietly in Jesus' presence with sweet fellowship, prayer and connection - total bliss. Then my friend said something that really bothered me. She said, "I hate that this sweet fellowship has to stop when I get up to get ready for the day." Even though that lunch was several years ago, those words still haunt and disturb me. They bother me because my friend had the mindset that just because she changes an activity, her communion with God has the same start and stop paradigm rather than being continuous. You see, from my perception, I don't think that my fellowship with God stops when I'm "done" praying in the morning. In my way of thinking, just because I get up from my "prayer chair" to go brush my teeth doesn't mean that my communion with Jesus has stopped, it's just changed to a different format. Sometimes my fellowship with Jesus continues through some Bible verses that I might be trying to memorize as I take my morning shower.

Consider this, let's not only have our morning prayer and quiet time with Jesus, but let's bring Jesus with us when we're getting breakfast and taking the kids to school - praying aloud on the way. Let's bring Jesus to our workplace or school, asking for His help with difficult people, impossible assignments, and overdue deadlines. When we're separating laundry, let's make mental piles that belong to Jesus (casting our cares on Him). Washing the dishes is a great opportunity to consider letting Jesus wash up some dirty or dark spots in our thinking, conversations and emotions. When you sit down to study for a class, consider asking Jesus to help you to understand and retain what you'll be studying and then thank Jesus for His help at the end of your study time. Let's bring Jesus to lunch and maybe even take one or two days a week to steal away for 10 minutes to talk with Jesus about what's happening. Let's whisper a quick thanks to Jesus for His help with a challenging situation that gets pleasantly resolved and even improved. When I'm figuring out what clothes to wear in the morning, I ask Jesus to help me because I'm not very good with fashion or style. (I think that clashing is another form of entertainment.)

Let's look for ways to integrate Jesus into our daily living, through prayer, fellowship, communion, asking Him for help, singing to him under our breath about our love for Him, shooting up a quick thanks for a good parking spot.

One of the most magnificent things to consider about Jesus is that He is *incarnate*. When Jesus came to the earth, the Son of God put on skin, took on a human existence like you and me and lived in the same 24 hour increments that we all experience. Jesus was fully God "as though He were not man and He was fully man as though He were not God." Jesus totally gets what it means to live a human life, with finite time, resources, energy, and with responsibilities, expectations, demands and pressures. When we think about integrating Jesus more fully into our daily living, there are a few authors who have spoken well about such integration. Consider reading, The Practice of God's Presence by Andrew Murray or Hearing God by Dallas Willard. Both of these gentlemen have some helpful insights about integrating our relationship and time with Jesus into our daily living, responsibilities, and activities.

With all of those suggestions, I pray that Jesus will spark your creativity to look for even more ways to integrate Him into your daily living - maybe even post a few suggestions on my Facebook wall to help others in this adventure as well! Integration is a far better strategy than separation when it comes to Jesus in our daily living-notwithstanding the importance of occasional retreats, vacations, and God getaways. I think that Jesus' answer to Martha provides some really good insight to His values and the importance of maintaining a healthy, dynamic, and vibrant relationship with Jesus! Luke 10:41-42:

41 *"Martha, Martha, you are worried and bothered about so many things;*
42 *but only one thing is necessary, for Mary has chosen the good part, which shall not be taken away from her."*

The next occasion where we read about Martha is in John 11 when she and Mary summon Jesus to come and heal their brother, Lazarus, who was very sick. When they requested Jesus to come, He was in a distant village at least 1-2 days walk away from Bethany, where they lived (no bullet train, FaceTime, Skype, Concorde jet, or text messaging back in the day). The strange thing about this whole situation is that Jesus waited on purpose where He was until Lazarus was dead before He decided to pop over to Bethany. If you're in the shoes of Martha and Mary, the longer Jesus the takes to arrive in Bethany and do His healing thing, the more impatient Martha and Mary become because they see their brother's health deteriorate hour by hour, day after day, until it's too late and Lazarus dies. Finally, when Jesus shows up, we get to see an interesting conversation transpire between him and Martha.

On a quick side note, please remember that when we first met Martha, she was in super octane "hostess mode" with her request to Jesus to make Mary help her. Jesus dialed Martha back and helped her understand that being in a relationship with Him was not "wasted time." In John 11 when we meet Martha, she's abandoned her hostess mode (even though there were many Jews at her house to help console Martha and Mary with the death of their brother, Lazarus) and left everyone at her house to go outside of Bethany to meet up with Jesus. In John 11:20-22 it says,

20 *"Martha therefore, when she heard that Jesus was coming, went to meet Him, but Mary stayed at the house.*

21 *Martha then said to Jesus, "Lord, if You had been here, my brother would not have died.*

22 *"Even now I know that whatever You ask of God, God will give You."*

I think that her behavior shows that she's adjusted her priorities and made them to align better with what Jesus was talking about in Luke 10:41-42.

With that being said, an interesting conversation develops between Martha and Jesus. Right out of the gate, Martha expresses that if

Jesus would have been around, Lazarus would not have died. This perception was 100% true in both the minds of Martha and Mary (John 11:32). This was the first thing that both of these sisters said to Jesus when they see Him, several days after they had initially summoned Him. Even though Martha leads with this statement, "If you'd been here, my brother would not have died", she doesn't stop the conversation at that point - unlike Mary. Martha continues in a really cool discussion with Jesus and the topic of resurrection comes up in the conversation, with Martha readily acknowledging that Jesus could ask anything from God and God would do it for Him. In this conversation, Martha gets to know Jesus better than she did before they had this discussion - all as a consequence of her brother's death. At one point, Jesus even tells Martha that He is the resurrection and the life (John 11:21-27). Martha doesn't let the grief and loss of her brother undermine her relationship with Jesus. In contrast, when Martha finishes her conversation with Jesus, she goes and tells Mary that Jesus is asking after her and Mary quickly gets up, runs out to Jesus, falls at His feet weeping and says, "If you'd been here, my brother would not have died."

Both sisters were of course very upset that their brother had died. Both were going through their experiences with grief and both had pinned a massive amount of hope on Jesus that He would come and heal their brother so he wouldn't die. So in their own way, they were probably disappointed with Jesus for being *too late.* In Martha's grief, she talks with Jesus and gets closer to Him through her conversation. In Mary's grief, she falls at Jesus' feet weeping and we know of no further discussion between Jesus and Mary besides Mary's observation about Jesus being too late. In this situation, Martha made the better choice than Mary. Martha held onto Jesus more than her emotions and grief. As a result, we see that Martha was with Jesus when He raised Lazarus from the dead (John 11:39-44), experiencing firsthand what Jesus was talking about when He told her that He was the resurrection and the life. In contrast, the only thing we read about Mary in this situation is that she fell at Jesus feet crying, disappointed, probably frustrated, and maybe a little bitter. We don't know if Mary saw her brother raised from the dead, like Martha her sister.

Even though Martha messed up her priorities in her first meeting with Jesus, this second interaction with Jesus turned out much better for her than the first go around. To begin, Martha made the right choice to drop the super octane hostess mode and leave her house full of guests to go out and be with Jesus. Second, Martha made the right decision to not let her emotions control her closeness to Jesus. Yes, she was disappointed that Jesus hadn't shown up in time, but she didn't allow her disappointment with Jesus to poison her intimacy with Him. Finally, Martha made the right choice not to press the stench problem too much when Jesus requested that the stone be removed from Lazarus' tomb. Even though Martha's personality was such that she was concerned about the dead body odor from her brother, she didn't throw down and accuse Jesus of going too far with his request at the tomb. Let's let Jesus be Jesus, even when we have to make our personalities take a back seat to His requests. When it's all said and done, we just might get to know Jesus better than we had ever anticipated. Martha saw firsthand her brother, Lazarus, raised from the dead and I believe this experience entirely revolutionized her life - all because she made better decisions. Remember that Martha and Mary were thinking of healing when they asked Jesus to come when Lazarus was sick. In contrast, Jesus was thinking of resurrection when he waited until Lazarus died before he went to Bethany.

The last time we read about Martha is in the following chapter, John 12. After Jesus had raised Lazarus from the dead, Martha, Mary, and Lazarus had Jesus over for dinner again, similar to the meal in Luke 10 when we first met these sisters. Only this time, the relationship this family had with Jesus had considerably deepened. They had worked through disappointment, discouragement, death, correction, grief, and even experienced the miracle of resurrection. So when Jesus comes to their house for dinner this night, it wasn't in the rigid formal introduction mode that we saw in Luke 10, with His first meal there. Rather, this meal was almost like a family homecoming and you can see this level of closeness among them by the respective ways that they behaved at this meal. John 12:2 says that Lazarus was reclining at the table with Jesus, the normal style of eating at this time and in this culture. Mary was again at Jesus feet, anointing them with costly perfume and drying his feet with her hair, John 12:3. And Martha was back to her normal serving mode, John 12:2. Although Martha and Mary were back in the same places they were when we first met them in Luke 10, they were both very changed because of the depth of relationship they had experienced with Jesus in their unique ways and personalities. Let's learn from Martha and make decisions in concert with knowing Jesus more and more, better and better each day. Who knows? We just might experience some resurrection in areas that we had thought were good and dead, hopeless beyond all human efforts.

Consider a few of the following action points that could be helpful:

- In what ways could you be like Martha, perhaps getting trapped in the quagmires of busyness and achievement?

- In what ways could you make better decisions to facilitate a deeper relationship with Jesus?

- Make a list of some areas in your life that need resurrection.

MODERNEXAMPLE

Please remember that this section isn't designed to show you a perfect person but rather an inspiring woman who had some amazing moments and achievements. As you read about her, consider how God could work in your life to help you be a Jesus Chick.

HENRIETTA LACKS

We live in a very medically advanced world, where scientists have used human cells to do research, make improvements, and even discover cures for all kinds of maladies. Scientists have used human cells in their efforts to map genetic structures, do cancer research, study the effects of toxins and radiation, and much more. It's really interesting that the person's whose cells have been used by literally thousands of scientists throughout the world, were from a woman we know as Henrietta Lacks.

Henrietta was born in 1921 in Virginia into a poor African American family. Her mother died when she was four and Henrietta moved into the log cabin where her grandfather lived which was the slave quarters on a white plantation. Henrietta had her first child when she was fourteen and had four more children before she died of cancer at the age of 31. While the doctors were treating Henrietta's cancer, they removed some cervical cells from her, without her knowledge. These cells were given to a researcher who was able to isolate and grow one cell into a whole strand of cells that have ultimately been reproduced and used for many medical studies and advances throughout the world.

Even though Henrietta's earthly life was filled with hardship, pain, disappointments, and struggles, her cells live today and have given life because of the research and knowledge gained from them to help millions of people around the world for many decades. Henrietta's life is a really amazing example of resurrection!

CHAPTER 5
GENEROSITY
Widow's Mite

When my husband and I were first married we had some interesting discussions about money. I'll never forget the conversation when he gave me four amortization schedules for different loan configurations and he wanted me to study these schedules and give him my feedback. First off, I had no earthly clue what that schedule thing was and it just looked like four stacks of papers with lots of numbers on them. I could tell by his tone that this was important to him, so I figured that I should start with the obvious, "What's an amor-whatever schedule?" He graciously explained that each group of papers gave a detailed monthly account of the principle, interest, insurance, etc of a loan configuration at various rates and over the course of various amounts of time. As I flipped through the pages for a quick overview, I found a page that had some random month, in some random year where it stated how much of the monthly mortgage would be paid to principle, etc. I felt relatively comfortable that I understood in theory the reams of paper that I was holding, but more importantly to me, I was concerned about my husband's mind frame with the decision to potentially buy a house. At the time, he was an electrical engineer with a stable job and we were renting a two bedroom apartment. As I was reading his body language, it was easy to see that he was <u>extremely</u> stressed out about this decision and I wanted to understand his concerns first before I started giving amor-whatever feedback. As we talked about the possibility of buying this house, he explained that it made him quite nervous to take out a loan for the most amount of money he had ever borrowed in his entire life. This was a really big decision for him and he didn't want to mess it up! I quickly replied that I would prefer to live with him in the two bedroom rented apartment and have him be happy and settled rather than buy a house and have him be constantly jittery and stressed. In my thinking, happiness is more related to the choices that we make rather than the money in our wallets.

Money is a big deal in our world and the truth of it is that money has always been something important from the beginning of mankind. We use money for all kinds of purposes from grocery shopping, to credit card purchases on the web, to giving a homeless person a few dollars to paying college tuition, and much more. Money has also been used to "buy" fame, power, influence, significance, leadership, beauty, intelligence, and many other intangible goods. If we aren't careful, we also give money great power when it becomes the primary pursuit in our lives.

In Jesus' day, people had many of the same challenges with money that we face today - what's enough, how to use our money well, saving, spending, taxes, inflation, religious and charitable giving, inheritances, investments, etc.

In Jesus' day, there were very rich people, middle class people, and very poor people, just like we have in our modern world. And thankfully, Jesus didn't keep quiet on the topic of money. In fact, during Jesus' earthly visit, He spoke about it very frequently. For example, if you think about it, His parables about the hidden treasure, pearl of great price, sower and the seed, lost coin, good Samaritan and others all have important applications for us including how we use our money. Furthermore, Jesus was betrayed for money and maybe some of that still happens today. Maybe we have betrayed Jesus so that we could get more money - just something to consider.

Nevertheless, Jesus not only gave parables about money, but he also said many important things about money in His various teachings:

- the Sermon on the Mount in Matthew 6:2-4
- answering the religious leaders about paying taxes in Mark 12:14-17
- His discussion with the rich young ruler in Matthew 19:16-26

These passages and the parable examples give some really hefty content for us to digest and absorb from Jesus' direct teaching.

As a stark and simple contrast, however, there's a situation related to money with a woman that requires our attention when we are talking about Jesus Chicks. In Mark 12:41-44, we read:

41 *"And He sat down opposite the treasury, and began observing how the people were putting money into the treasury; and many rich people were putting in large sums. 42 A poor widow came and put in two small copper coins, which amount to a cent. 43 Calling His disciples to Him, He said to them, "Truly I say to you, this poor widow put in more than all the contributors to the treasury; 44 for they all put in out of their surplus, but she, out of her poverty, put in all she owned, all she had to live on."* (NASU)

In these three verses (also detailed in Luke 21:1-4), Jesus packs a whallop! To begin, it's important to understand the context and background of what Jesus says. First of all, we read in Mark that Jesus sat down opposite the treasury in the Temple. At this time in history, the treasury was probably the name given to the area that was known as the Court of Women, where there were 13 boxes or chests called "trumpets" whose openings were shapes like funnels. Historians say that a person who was making a financial gift would come to the Court of Women and throw their donation into one of these boxes. Rather than passing a bucket, a plate or a bag, or rather than setting donation boxes on walls, like we do in today's churches, in Jesus' day receiving offerings seemed to be a little more simple but not limited to a formal church service or a certain time during a church service. Maybe things were less complicated then - no texting to give, web donations, credit card processing, tax credits, end of year receipts, etc.

As a contrast, however, when you read in Mark 12:41, it's quite obvious that Jesus was watching *how* the people were giving and seeing the many rich people put in large sums of money. Just this sentence alone makes my intestines twist. We have to seriously stop and consider that Jesus was watching every single person that was giving: He watched *how* they gave and He watched *what* they gave. If we role this into our modern living, I know many people who would get completely stressed out if what they gave and how they gave was publicly known, to say nothing of the challenge they would have hearing Jesus give a commentary on their giving! And yet, that is exactly what Jesus was doing in these verses. What Jesus did in His day would be like Him watching me put my money in our offering bucket during the offering and then talking with His disciples about how I gave (was I stingy, generous, joyful, cranky, apathetic, worshipful, etc) and the amount that I gave. If this happened in our churches today, let me just say that more than a few people would break out in a sweat, to put it mildly.

This act is very interesting to me. Jesus chose a seat opposite the offering boxes so He could watch everyone give and see how much they gave. None of what He did or said was coincidental or whimsical. Knowing that He was on borrowed time, so to speak, everything Jesus said and did was filled with meaning and application. So when Jesus spotlights the poor widow's giving, it's a clarion call to us to zero in and pay attention, particularly with Jesus accentuating the contrasts between this poor widow and her wealthy counterparts. I think it's really powerful that Jesus singles out this poor woman for how little she gave, particularly when you read the contrast about how the wealthy people were putting in large sums of money. Human conditioning says that more is better, but in this situation from Jesus' estimation, there's a discrepancy. The widow's paltry giving is exalted in contrast to the profuse offering of the wealthy. In fact, Jesus is so impressed with this widow's generosity that He calls over His disciples to focus their attention on not only what the woman gave, but more importantly, *how* she gave. Jesus says about this woman in Mark 12:43-44, *". . . . this poor widow put in more than all the contributors to the treasury;* 44 *for they all put in out of their surplus, but she, out of her poverty, put in all she owned, all she had to live on."*

This poor widow was sacrificial in her giving and it came out of her deep relationship with and respect for God. The wealthy donors, on the other hand, gave from a more religious mindset with an unspoken expectation of reciprocity. The wealthy people at Jesus' time gave to receive recognition, honor, respect, and admiration. What captured Jesus' attention and applause wasn't the huge quantities of money the wealthy people could afford to give, but what the poor marginalized widow couldn't afford to give, but did nevertheless. This poor, nameless widow arrested Jesus' focus not because of the amount that she gave, but more so the totality of how she gave. How many lessons and applications can we work into our lives from her example?!

When we think about it, how we use our money speaks volumes about what our priorities are and even more about who we are as people. Furthermore, let me also propose to you that in our modern living, time is possibly a more valued commodity than money - a person can earn more money, but we don't have the ability to earn or make more time. Each human receives the daily gift of 24 hours (unless you're traveling internationally and then everything gets messed up). How do we use our time and our money? The religious mindset sees money and time with a reciprocity perspective. Religion is just another tool, method or means to acquire power, influence, admiration, perceived significance, etc. In contrast, the relational mindset says that money and time are resources to be sacrificed for a deeper connection and relationship with our Beloved. Truly, when we are committed to love, then money and time become expressions and conduits for that love. So let's take this poor widows challenge to love sacrificially with our money and time.

To finish the story with which I began this chapter, my husband and I carefully looked at our expenses and revenue to formulate a reasonable budget that worked for us. We moved forward with buying the house and learned some valuable take-aways about managing our money, being frugal, saving, investing, maintenance, car insurance (another story for another book), teamwork, do-it-yourself home projects (or not), along with many other newlywed lessons. Buying the house wasn't nearly as important as learning the lessons I just listed. Maybe it's kind of along the same lines that Jesus was expressing with his disciples that the quantity of the money isn't as important as the state of the heart.

Consider a few of the following action points that could be helpful:

- Think about how you spend your money and time. Do these "expenditures" accurately reflect the priorities you profess?

- List three of the most important lessons in your life that you've learned about money?

- List several ways that you could be more sacrificial with your money time.

  Below are a few ideas for you to consider doing:

- Volunteering: at a local school, giving literacy lessons in a prison, church greeter or small group person, or joining a Saving Moses international team trip.

- Giving money: Samaritans Purse with Operation Christmas Child, Saving Moses through NightCare and Malnutrition Clinics, percentage giving to your church, or donating to the kids' lemonade stand.

MODERNEXAMPLE

Please remember that this section isn't designed to show you a perfect person but rather an inspiring woman who had some amazing moments and achievements. As you read about her, consider how God could work in your life to help you be a Jesus Chick.

MOTHER TERESA

One of my all-time favorite modern heroes is Mother Teresa. While her accomplishments over the course of several decades have given her worldwide acclaim and recognition, what continually captures my heart about her is her total and utter devotion to Jesus. Mother Teresa was a very small Albanian nun who said "yes" to Jesus and maintained that "yes" regardless of how she felt, what she went through, who she touched, or how she was received. What has only become recently known is that Mother Teresa served the majority of her time with the Missionaries of Charity in what she called "spiritual darkness". Even though she received her call into her unique ministry through a very strong and profound experience with Jesus, she didn't continue to have the rich encounter with Jesus from this initial call. Instead, she went about her call and work giving all of her small body and existence as fully as she possibly could to serving Jesus by helping the poor. One of my favorite things that she said was, "I'm a little pencil in the hand of a writing God, who is sending a love letter to the world." Mother Teresa inspires me to give everything that I have out of my love for Jesus, even if it doesn't seem very big. Mother Teresa had small stature with small beginnings from a very small country but her life demonstrated extravagant generosity.

CHAPTER 6
PROMISES
Mary, Mother of Jesus: Part 1

"Do you pinkie promise with no fingers crossed?" Perhaps when you were growing up, this was part of the regular elementary school vocabulary on the playground during recess. I remember doing that whole promise routine with different kids in my class and what I didn't realize at the time, but I now know, is that the strength of the promise is based on the character of the one doing the promising. Sketchy character = sketchy promise; strong character = strong promise. Having experienced both the sketchy and the strong, I choose strong over sketchy all the time and maybe this is one of the reasons I am such a Jesus freak, because of His strong character and consequently, His strong promises. Keeping promises is important and no one is better at keeping promises than God. Nevertheless, sometimes when we hear about what God promises, it's easy to feel like they're impossible, but let's be careful not to forget that character is an essential ingredient to keeping one's promise and in this light, God's character is the golden standard, so to speak.

Impossible Promises:
Sometimes you may hear God's promise that He will take care of your finances. When you first hear that promise and you look at your checkbook, the credit card bills, the debt that you've accumulated, all the payments due, and you hear the creditors calling and see the e-mails, it can be overwhelming. In contrast, God says: I will supply all of your needs according to my riches in glory (Philippians 4:17). When you hear the promise, sometimes it seems impossible. Maybe in the area of health, you look at your physical well-being and perhaps the doctors have said some rather discouraging things or made some extremely disheartening diagnosis. But in contrast, God says that He will give you health, long life, vitality, length of days and strength. When you hear the promise, sometimes it seems impossible based on how you feel and what you hear. Sometimes, God's promises seem impossible.

To look at a real life example of the promise challenge, let's consider the life of Mary, the mother of Jesus, starting with her introduction in the Gospels and her life before Jesus' birth. Mary's life is a really interesting experience when you consider what she went through in the light of God's promises to her. The beginning introduction to Mary's life can be read in Matthew 1, but the most content about this part of Mary's life can be found in Luke 1. In Luke 1:28, Gabriel comes to Mary and says, "Greetings favored one! The Lord is with you." With this salutation, let's try to understand a little bit around who Mary was when Gabriel spoke to her at this time.

Mary is a teenage girl and not married. In her culture, it was normal for her to live with her parents and probably from the time she was around 5 to 10 years old, she was promised or engaged to Joseph by her father. Until she became married, she would not live with Joseph based on the social norms of her day. Furthermore, in this culture, there was a definite protocol for proper gender relationships. Women obviously could talk with women and chat it up and have no problems. And in the same way, men would talk with other men. It was, however, completely inappropriate and unacceptable for a man to talk with a woman especially a strange man and especially a teenage girl who's promised in marriage to another guy. So the angel Gabriel, who was probably a big guy and not a chunky little cherub with wings, shows up on the scene and says, "Hey Mary! You are highly favored!" Her reaction says it all, "She was perplexed and pondered." Gabriel continues his conversation and says, "Don't be afraid", implying that she was afraid and rightfully so. Mary didn't have a lot of interaction with strange men and Gabriel pops up and starts talking to her, and she's a little jittery and nervous about this weird and chatty guy. It's easy to see why she might have thought, "What's he trying to do? What's going on here? This is too strange."

Rather than getting sidetracked with answering Mary's questions and curiosities, Gabriel stays on target with his assignment and explains to Mary in Luke 1:30-33:

30 *Do not be afraid, Mary; for you have found favor with God.* 31 *"And behold, you will conceive in your womb and bear a son, and you shall name Him Jesus.* 32 *"He will be great and will be called the Son of the Most High; and the Lord God will give Him the throne of His father David;* 33 *and He will reign over the house of Jacob forever, and His kingdom will have no end."*

Gabriel announces to a teenage girl, unmarried, "Guess what?! You're going to get pregnant - lucky you!" It's hard for me to imagine what was running through Mary's thoughts at just that moment.

Maybe she thought, "Say what?! Are you serious?! And just WHO ARE YOU?!" But what Mary says tells a lot about who she is. In Luke 1:34, Mary says, "How can this be since I am a virgin?" And basically what she's saying is, "That's impossible. My mom told me how you get pregnant and I've never done that so it's impossible." I don't think she said this with unbelief. I think she said this with innocence and there's a difference.

Here's an important take away for us with how Mary responded to Gabriel's presentation. Mary's reaction didn't portray unbelief, doubt, scorn or arrogant rejection just because Gabriel's words seemed impossible. The same challenge exists for us today in relation to God's promises. We can be doubtful, skeptical, suspicious, cynical, sarcastic, and snarky - all various forms of unbelief. Or we can say to God's promises, "Wow! That's amazing! I don't totally understand, but I'm eager to learn and discover through the journey." One reaction can be naïve like Mary or the other stuck in unbelief. This is a real challenge for us today in relation to God's promises. But I want to encourage you that God's promises in your life are not impossible. I don't think Mary's question to Gabriel was rooted in unbelief, but rather in innocence. And Gabriel's answer speaks to Mary's innocent question. Gabriel says in Luke 1:35, *"The Holy Spirit will come upon you, and the power of the Most High will overshadow you; and for that reason the Holy Child shall be called the Son of God."*

How Mary responds to Gabriel is one of the most practical and yet profound answers that I challenge myself to live every day. In Luke 1:38, Mary says, *"Behold, the bond slave of the Lord; may it be done to me according to your word."* In my way of thinking, Mary models for us the right answer to God's promises: may it be done to me according to Your word. So be it. You said it. May it be the way you said. That's exactly the right answer. Sometimes we need to coach ourselves to give the right answer. For example, with my kids when I ask them to do something, I don't expect them to give me a snarky or cynical reply. I expect them to answer with a respectful affirmation. Sometimes, I get to coach them a little, to peel back some attitude, but this helps me to think about how I respond to God speaking into my life. While I don't believe that God made us to be robots and to chime off pad answers and replies, there's also a place in our relationship with God where we decide to believe God's word, trust God's promises and affirm God's leadership in our lives. The right answer to God's promises in our lives is, "Let it be done to me as You say."

Sometimes we need to be coached with the right answer. Even as adults, God coaches us. The right answer is "let it be done as you say." Let's practice that today. Say it with me: Let it be done as you say. That's the right answer with God's promises for your impossibility. Let it be done as you say, but watch this. Because as you continue on, the angel continues to encourage Mary and Mary has some challenges in front of her. She takes a step in essence. She says ok, it's impossible but the right answer "let it be done as you say."

Improbable Promises:
Once we get the right answer locked into place in our lives as Mary did, we make the next step with God's promises from impossible to improbable, meaning that you've decided that God's promises are not impossible, even though they may seem unlikely. They're not impossible but just improbable. Now let's consider why this was unlikely, difficult, or challenging for Mary. Mary is a single, but engaged, teenage girl who lives with her mom and dad. She's probably never lived away from home and an angel comes and tells her you're going to get pregnant. With this kind of information, it's obvious that she has some hurdles in front of her that she must consider.

- Challenge number one: the physical challenge, "I've never known a guy in that way. Ok check that one off. The angel took care of that one and answered it.

- Challenge number two: What about Mary's family? What's going to happen to her when she's pregnant out of wedlock? How's that going to go over with mom and dad? "Guess what mom and dad, this angel came to me and told me I'm going to be pregnant. Isn't that exciting? Where's Joseph? Well he said don't worry about Joseph. The angel said it's going to be a supernatural pregnancy." Think if you're the mom and dad and you get that message. Really? God would have to coach you on the right words to say because the normal parental reaction to this kind of information at that time was to ostracize the unwed mother. The best that could happen would be that Mary was left alone and pushed outside of society.

- Challenge number three: the religious norms and culture in this society and at this time required all women who became pregnant out of wedlock to be stoned to death. That was normal and definitely a challenge.

- Challenge number four: the actual physical pregnancy. Remember, if Mary is ostracized and pushed outside of society there's no familial or relational support. When I think back about the first time I was pregnant, it was a pretty steep learning curve - pretty much vertical for me.

The first time I was pregnant, I remember thinking, "Thank God we have 9 months to think about this whole transition and try to figure out what we're doing!" In the first three months, the first trimester, I was a little uncomfortable, maybe a little nauseous. Thankfully, I had lots of friends around me and a great doctor to give me practical advice and helpful suggestions - drink lots of water, eat crackers, take your prenatal vitamins, eat raw almonds, get rest, etc. Then I remember going to the doctor and hearing my daughter's heartbeat (even though it was too early to know she was a girl). That's so exciting! How cool is that?! In the second trimester, I started to feel my daughter moving and that was completely incredible! In the third trimester, I was kind of tired and had difficulty sleeping. Throughout my entire first pregnancy, I had a really strong support network around me filled with fantastic medical care, wonderful friends, and my caring family. Even with all of this amazing help, it was still a 100% vertical learning curve, fantastic but vertical. In contrast to my experience, it's difficult for me to imagine what it was like for Mary to be pregnant in the context of her culture, social norms, and religious traditions - an unwed pregnant teenager.

Perhaps this was partly why God locked into place the helpful information from Gabriel that Elizabeth, Mary's cousin, was pregnant despite being past the age of child bearing. I love that God's promises are accompanied by God's help and coaching all along the way! Gabriel tells Mary in Luke 1:36 that Elizabeth was already six months pregnant, partially to encourage Mary that nothing is impossible with God, but also possibly to give some help to both Mary and Elizabeth who found themselves in relatively impossible situations. In Luke 1:39, we read that Mary hurried down to stay with Elizabeth.

Now let's think about this. We have Mary, who now has some relational support by going to connect with Elizabeth and this gets really exciting. When Mary arrived, Elizabeth's husband, Zacharias greets Mary, "Hey there, Mary, nice to see you." I'm sure that Mary was really glad to visit Elizabeth, probably even eager. Perhaps she said to Zacharias, "I hear that Elizabeth's pregnant!" Elizabeth comes bounding on the scene and is so excited! She exclaims in Luke 1:43-44, *"How is it that the mother of my Lord is come to visit me? The baby inside of me was leaping with joy when he heard your voice - I'm so thrilled that you are here!"* That's how Elizabeth responded when Mary came knocking at their door.

Do you realize that Mary didn't have to tell Elizabeth that she was pregnant? Elizabeth told Mary. There's a good probability that Mary felt some shame from being pregnant out of wedlock. I think she was excited when an angel came and told her that her pregnancy was very supernatural, but maybe she didn't feel very comfortable telling her mom and dad about being pregnant because that could turn out bad and it was likely that she didn't tell her friends because if the word got out, really bad things could happen. Nevertheless, Mary had this extremely big news, but who could she safely tell her news? How was it that she didn't even have to tell Elizabeth! Elizabeth tells Mary and she is so excited that Mary has come to visit - so thrilling! This must have been a tremendous relief to Mary. Whew! "The cat's out of the bag - secret's out. I don't have to get nervous and scared about what's going to happen or worried about my immediate future." Elizabeth already knows - she told Mary because God told her. How cool that God provided the relational support that both of these women needed at this very important juncture of their lives!

Let's pause for a minute from Mary and consider Elizabeth and what she's going through at this time. Elizabeth, who's in her older years, is pregnant for the first time. If you think about this, she's already been pregnant for six months and when you're pregnant for the first time, you have a lot of questions and by the time you get to the third trimester, you've got six months under your belt, so to speak. You're also pretty tired, the longer you're pregnant. When you add in that Elizabeth is an older pregnant lady, she's all the more tired. I bring out these points because Mary arriving at Elizabeth's house when she does was very fortuitous timing. From Mary's perspective, she had a lot of questions. "What happens at this time? What should I expect to feel and experience the longer I'm pregnant? How can I tell when my baby is moving? If I have morning sickness, what are some helpful suggestions?" When I was pregnant with my first child, I remember the first time they told me that she was moving but I just thought that my stomach was feeling a little queasy. Thankfully, Elizabeth could coach Mary through the lion's share of her new experiences having just gone through the same stuff a few weeks and months earlier. Perhaps some of what Elizabeth said to Mary, "Now Mary you're going to feel like you have to use the bathroom more and your clothes are going to get a little tight. Mary you might not feel real well the first couple of months here and you'll need to drink a lot of water. I know all of this because I just did 6 months of doing all this stuff. I know what it's going to feel like when you transition into the second trimester. You're going to have more energy."

So Elizabeth is in a really good place to give Mary almost real-time coaching through all this stuff. Isn't God efficient? He absolutely takes Mary, a teenage girl, pregnant out of wedlock and helps her walk through this transition. But let's also consider Elizabeth for a little bit. As we think about Mary who is a teenage girl, likely with lots of energy, we also have Elizabeth who doesn't have nearly the energy that Mary has. Elizabeth is older and pregnant and in the last trimester of her pregnancy when you tend to get the most tired. Mary could have been a really big blessing in Elizabeth's life. Mary could come alongside Elizabeth and possibly help with the cooking for the day. Maybe Mary said to Elizabeth, "Why don't you sit down and relax. I'll go ahead and take care of getting the water. I'll do the laundry. I'll do the dishes. I'll clean the house. I can be a great blessing to you. I know you're tired. I know you're kind of on the older end of things and I know you're in your last trimester and I'm here. I've got lots of energy and I can be a resource to you. Let me be a complement. Let me help you as much as you're helping me." What a fantastic fit God made between these two women! While God's promises at first seem impossible, when you start to take some steps then they become just a little less impossible.

As you walk through this journey with these women, not only did Elizabeth have help from Mary and Mary have help from Elizabeth, but in Matthew 1:18 and following, it says that when Joseph found out that Mary was pregnant he was going to put her to the side quietly but God gave him a dream. God said the baby in her womb is a very supernatural baby and He has a divine purpose and a plan. God let Joseph know in that dream that He wanted him to be a father to that baby and to take Mary as his wife - protect her, watch over her and be a covering for her. So when Mary comes home after three months of staying with Elizabeth, she connects with Joseph and he's prepared to help Mary go through this journey with dignity, protection and grace. Joseph knows that she's pregnant but he takes care of her. He remains committed to Mary as her husband and gives security and safety. His actions said to Mary, "We're going to have this baby together and we're going to raise Him as His mom and a dad. I know He's supernatural and I'm here to be a resource and a covering of protection to you." This is what I want to encourage you with: line upon line, step by step, God's promises become increasingly less and less impossible and more and more incarnate. This means that God's promises become a reality. Jesus became incarnate.

Incarnate Promises:

When we say that Jesus became incarnate, this means that the son of God sitting at the right hand of God the Father comes down to the earth, takes on human flesh and form and walks among us fully God as though He were not man and fully man as though He were not God. God's promises become incarnate, moving from impossible to improbable and from improbable to incarnate. Here's some really good application that we can take into our daily living, from watching Mary and how she handled this whole pregnancy challenge. When something that God says to us seems impossible, just like Mary, may our first answer to impossible be what Mary said, "Let it be according to your word." Let our reaction to God be, "Whatever you say God, I believe it - I'm on board with you and I'm on your page. I'm a believer and not a doubter. While what you say may seem impossible, I choose to trust you. I know that nothing is impossible with you based on Luke 1:37."

After we take this step, then our second answer to when God's promises seem improbable, is to take another step, moving from impossible towards incarnate, one step at a time, like Mary. She went to visit Elizabeth, received some encouragement from her time there, and then took another step. When Mary gets home, she connects with Joseph whom God has already prepared to help Mary along this very supernatural journey. Once we decide to believe and trust in God's promises, even though they seem impossible, the next part of the journey moves away from impossible and becomes improbable. If you notice Mary's pregnancy journey, she doesn't give birth at home, but rather in Bethlehem, the city of Joseph's family heritage. Having met up with Joseph upon her return, she gets on a donkey and rides between four days and up to possibly a week, on a donkey to register for the census in Bethlehem that Caesar Augustus has commanded throughout the Roman Empire. If you think about it, the last thing you want to do in your final days of being pregnant is to ride on a donkey on a dirty, bumpy, rickety road. By this point, Mary is probably waddling. In the final days of being pregnant, the baby drops down closer to being delivered and Mary can mostly likely tell that Jesus' arrival is getting really close.

And how about Joseph? What does he know? He's a carpenter. He doesn't even have sheep and probably lacks any previous practice to have an inkling of what's happening with his wife and how to deliver a baby. When Joseph and Mary arrive in Bethlehem, because there was no room in the inn, they wind up staying in a barn. If you think about it, a barn was the dirtiest, grossest, and possibly most unclean place where Mary could deliver a baby. In Mary's culture it was very improper for a man to participate with a woman's delivery - the men were generally not allowed in the delivery room, so they were kept off to the side and for all we know, Mary, a teenage girl, delivered Jesus all by herself. Of course we don't know for certain, but what we do know is that once she delivers Jesus, whom we know as the Son of God, the first bed he lays in is a feeding trough for animals - a manger.

Take just a minute and think about this: here is the incarnation, the actual physical presence of the Promise of God that went back 2 millennia to Genesis 3:15 and 16 when God promised Adam and Eve, "...your son will crush the head of the serpent," going through fourteen generations up to King David and fourteen more generations up to Joseph now in Bethlehem and here is the Son of God. This whole promise, this thread of a promise that goes through the entire Old Testament now suddenly becomes a reality by a teenage unwed mother whose answer to impossible was simply put, "So be it." Perhaps all of that is a challenge to us that if Mary with all of these difficulties, hardships, uncertainties, impossibilities, and improbabilities could say "so be it", maybe she can be a tangible example to us of God's promises in our life and how we can answer to those promises. When God's promises seem impossible, the right answer is, "Let it be according to your word." When God's promises seem improbable, the right answer is, "I'm going to take one step at a time." And when God's promises become incarnate the right answer is, "Let's worship and celebrate!"

When you think about it, Mary's in this barn and these random, unknown shepherds enter in on a very sacred moment.
In Luke 2:8-16 we read,

8 *In the same region there were some shepherds staying out in the fields and keeping watch over their flock by night.*

9 *And an angel of the Lord suddenly stood before them, and the glory of the Lord shone around them; and they were terribly frightened.*

10 *But the angel said to them, "Do not be afraid; for behold, I bring you good news of great joy which will be for all the people;*

11 *for today in the city of David there has been born for you a Savior, who is Christ the Lord.*

12 *"This will be a sign for you: you will find a baby wrapped in cloths and lying in a manger."*

13 *And suddenly there appeared with the angel a multitude of the heavenly host praising God and saying,*

14 *"Glory to God in the highest,*
And on earth peace among men with whom He is pleased."

15 *When the angels had gone away from them into heaven, the shepherds began saying to one another, "Let us go straight to Bethlehem then, and see this thing that has happened which the Lord has made known to us."*

16 *So they came in a hurry and found their way to Mary and Joseph, and the baby as He lay in the manger.*

When I delivered my first baby, I wasn't eager to have strange men popping into my delivery room to celebrate the birth of my daughter, let alone strange, smelly men possibly in the middle of the night who could be just a little crazy! But this was Mary's experience. These shepherds found Mary and Joseph and they were super excited! "We know you just had a baby and we are so pumped! We saw these angels in the field and they were coming up and down in the sky and there was light everywhere with this booming voice for a massive announcement! We are so excited and we couldn't help it - we hurried to find you and you're here! Let's celebrate! The Savior is born!" When you think about this whole thing, it gives us a great model for how to respond when God's promises become a reality in our lives. Celebrate! Honor! Worship! Get excited! Be thrilled! Be ecstatic! If we can get excited for various sports teams, movie releases, political events, etc, how much more can we get excited for the promises of God when they become a reality in our lives?!

Consider a few of the following action points that could be helpful:

- Model the right answer like Mary: let it be according to Your word and speak life to the promises that God has put in your heart.

- Take one step at a time. When you think about it, pregnancy takes 9 months for a baby to be delivered and sometimes God's promises take a little bit of time to walk them out and see them become true in our lives. It's also really important to have good relational support around you. It's super valuable to have people around you who are going to encourage you to believe that God is going to absolutely do everything He's promised you.

- Maintain wonder and awe. If you watch Mary in Luke 2:19, Mary responded to all of these events by pondering these things in her heart: she watched, she listened and she paid attention to what was happening in her life. Let's be like Mary and keep a sense of awe and wonder. Let's ponder God's promises, considering what God is doing all around us and watch for God moving in your life.

CHAPTER 7
COMMITMENT
Mary, Mother of Jesus: Part 2

I have three wonderful children whom I deeply love. They are totally awesome and rock my world almost every day. Being their mom has been one of the most significant honors of my life and I'm totally head over heels in love with them! From the time I was aware that they were growing in me, I've been entirely smitten and I'd say that I generally know them pretty well. In my tummy, each of them were different and as babies, I could see their distinct personalities in the really early days of each of their lives. As they've grown over time, I've been super keen to be with them in their high points, during their low moments, helping with homework, consoling them with friend challenges, listening to frustrations, teaching them about cooking, values, saving money, the importance of attitudes and respect, taking them to doctor appointments, cheering for them at their athletic events, confronting them about disobedience and a host of other "mom stuff." I love being a mom - it takes my breath away!

As I think about Mary being Jesus' mom, I would suppose that she wasn't that different from each of us who are moms. I think she hated it if Jesus came crying to her with a skinned knee from falling down and she probably knew his preferences with her cooking and perhaps he held her hand as a little boy, as she walked to get water from a well near their home. We know that Jesus earthly father, Joseph, was a carpenter (Matthew 13:55) and it's likely that Jesus was trained by Joseph to be a carpenter as well, learning a craft so He could reasonably support His family. As Jesus became close to being a teenager, we first read about what it was like to be His mom when He was on the cusp of becoming an adult in His culture. In Luke 2:42-49, we see an interesting account of what it was like to be Jesus' parents. We read in these verses,

42 *And when He became twelve, they went up there according to the custom of the Feast;*

43 *and as they were returning, after spending the full number of days, the boy Jesus stayed behind in Jerusalem. But His parents were unaware of it,*

44 *but supposed Him to be in the caravan, and went a day's journey; and they began looking for Him among their relatives and acquaintances.*

45 *When they did not find Him, they returned to Jerusalem looking for Him.*

46 *Then, after three days they found Him in the temple, sitting in the midst of the teachers, both listening to them and asking them questions.*

47 *And all who heard Him were amazed at His understanding and His answers.*

48 *When they saw Him, they were astonished; and His mother said to Him, "Son, why have You treated us this way? Behold, Your father and I have been anxiously looking for You."*

49 *And He said to them, "Why is it that you were looking for Me? Did you not know that I had to be in My Father's house?"*

I can most certainly relate to Mary concerns. I've accidentally left one of my kids at church, thinking that my husband was bringing them home and he thought I was bringing them. Thankfully, we only live a quick ten minute drive from church, so it's nothing like the three day trauma that Mary experienced, looking throughout an entire city for her son. I have a vivid imagination and I don't even want to start considering what I would be thinking about over the course of three days. And having finally found Jesus in the temple, I can only imagine the stress in her voice with her question about why Jesus would treat his parents with such seeming disregard and disinterest. But Jesus' reply would catch me off guard and I wouldn't know how to answer his questions. "Mom, why were you looking for me? Didn't you all know that I'd be in my Father's house, the temple? Why didn't you check there first?" How do you answer this?

The next time we see Jesus interacting with his mom is really the beginning of Jesus' ministry and is found in John 2 with the wedding feast situation. For all practical purposes, Jesus' mom nudges Jesus forward with her statement about the lack of wine. In this dialogue, we see that Jesus is an adult and Mary puts Him on the spot and it doesn't seem like He's all too keen to oblige her pressure. They were at a wedding feast and the normal supply of wine that was customary for this kind of a celebration had run out, putting the master of the feast in a real predicament. Mary says that her son can help with this challenge. Watch the dialogue between Mary and Jesus with the subsequent action in John 2:3-10:

3 *When the wine ran out, the mother of Jesus said to Him, "They have no wine."*

4 *And Jesus said to her, "Woman, what does that have to do with us? My hour has not yet come."*

5 *His mother said to the servants, "Whatever He says to you, do it."*

6 *Now there were six stone waterpots set there for the Jewish custom of purification, containing twenty or thirty gallons each.*

7 *Jesus said to them, "Fill the waterpots with water." So they filled them up to the brim.*

8 *And He said to them, "Draw some out now and take it to the headwaiter." So they took it to him.*

9 *When the headwaiter tasted the water which had become wine, and did not know where it came from (but the servants who had drawn the water knew), the headwaiter *called the bridegroom,*

10 *and said to him, "Every man serves the good wine first, and when the people have drunk freely, then he serves the poorer wine; but you have kept the good wine until now."*

Clearly, Mary had a very clear sense that her son could do something helpful to resolve this shortage and having made her request, she made sure to follow up with the servants to encourage them to obey her son, even if it seemed crazy. "Whatever He says to do, do it." Mary models for us how to interact with Jesus, even when it seems illogical and maybe even nonsensical. I totally love that Mary's behavior encouraged others to obey Jesus! If we would see God's hand move in our lives, we must be committed to obey Jesus. Miracles are not only the *result* of obedience, but consider that it's also miraculous that we obey Jesus in the first place!

And thus begins Jesus' ministry, comprised of two to three years of completely amazing stuff!!! At one point during Jesus' ministry, in

Mark 3:31-35, we read:

31 *Then His mother and His brothers arrived, and standing outside they sent word to Him and called Him.*

32 *A crowd was sitting around Him, and they said to Him, "Behold, Your mother and Your brothers are outside looking for You."*

33 *Answering them, He said, "Who are My mother and My brothers?"*

34 *Looking about at those who were sitting around Him, He said, "Behold My mother and My brothers!*

35 *"For whoever does the will of God, he is My brother and sister and mother."*

As a mom, it could be easy to take offense at Jesus' words and think, "How dare that young man treat me, His mother, like everyone else!" But it's my sincere belief that Mary knew her son was very unique and had a purpose on earth dramatically different than anyone else. Indeed, it says four times when Jesus was young that either Mary "treasured" or Mary "pondered" these things in her heart. Truly, you can't raise a son like Jesus and not know there's something very unique and divine about Him. So maybe Mary wasn't offended with Jesus when He put her on the same level with other people who do God's will in Mark 3:35.

Now here's the part of exploring Mary's relationship with her son Jesus that totally breaks me down, Jesus' crucifixion. I honestly can't imagine what it would be like to watch my son be brutally beaten, scourged beyond human recognition, and crucified for public humiliation—to die a shameful, slow and humiliating death. I've been around moms who have lost their children and there's nothing that shreds me at such a deep level. Even as I write this, I'm undone and find it difficult to express the intensity of what I'm feeling. I think it would turn me inside out to watch my son die such in such a violent and savage way. Everything would come out of me - my heart, my tears, my breath, emotions, nerves, and wailing . . . everything. You probably wouldn't be able to recognize me because I would be such a complete and total wreck. Someone would probably have to hold me back because I would want to take my son's place - please hurt me before you hurt my son. And yet, we read in John 19:25-27, *"But standing by the cross of Jesus were His mother... 26 When Jesus then saw His mother, and the disciple whom He loved standing nearby, He said to His mother, "Woman, behold, your son!" 27 Then He said to the disciple, "Behold, your mother!" From that hour the disciple took her into his own household."* (NASU)

When Gabriel spoke to Mary in Luke 2:35, he said that a sword would also pierce Mary's soul. I believe this was a prophecy to Mary of what would happen to Jesus on the cross and how this would cut her to the core as well. Losing a child, regardless of their age, is arguably one of the worst experiences through which a person could live. I've watched moms and dads lose their son or daughter and the loss almost broke each parent beyond repair. This kind of loss is something that Mary experienced - pierced through her soul, with grief that is overwhelming.

I want to believe that the Holy Spirit was present to comfort Mary when she was standing at the cross watching her son die. I want to believe that the Holy Spirit gave her strength, consolation, and hope. I want to believe that Mary accepted the presence of the Holy Spirit to help her through this day and the time leading up to the resurrection. I can't imagine how Mary could make it one second at a time without the help of the Holy Spirit. Mary might have been part of the group that helped prepare Jesus' body for the tomb but when her Son rose from the dead, think about what a joyous moment this was for her! The last place we read about Mary is in Acts 1 where it explains that she stayed in the Upper Room with the rest of Jesus' followers, devoting themselves to prayer.

What a unique role that Mary, Jesus' mother, had. Consider how powerfully God used Mary's life to bring God to live in human flesh in the context of human history. Mary was a really amazing Jesus Chick!

MODERNEXAMPLE

Please remember that this section isn't designed to show you a perfect person but rather an inspiring woman who had some amazing moments and achievements. As you read about her, consider how God could work in your life to help you be a Jesus Chick.

AMY CARMICHAEL

Amy Carmichael was born in 1867 in Northern Ireland into a fairly wealthy Christian family. During her childhood, her father lost his fortune, died, and her family moved to Belfast. While living there, she started visiting slums and observing the horrific living and working conditions of the girls and women in these neighborhoods. She was moved with compassion from these observations along with many others and began to feel God stirring in her heart to become a missionary. She lived in Japan for a little over a year, but put her roots down in Southern India, where she lived for more than fifty years. During her life, she was known for many things, but one of the most outstanding things that captures my attention is how she worked tirelessly to rescue toddlers and children from being prostitutes at Hindu temples.

The first child that she rescued was named Preena and here is the beginning of Amy's amazing ministry in Southern India:

"One day Preena, a little Indian girl, was collecting water for the temple near where Amy was speaking. Preena stopped to listen as Amy told the ladies about her God who loved everybody the same. He did not put people in different classes as the Indian caste system did. Preena was very interested in what Amy was saying but knew she must not be seen listening to the stranger. She tucked Amy's words into her memory and hurried back to the temple.

Indian girls were often unwanted and were given to the temple to serve as prostitutes. Because of this, when Preena arrived at Amy's door, Amy knew she could not send her back. The little girl would be beaten, even killed, if she were returned. Amy could have been charged with kidnapping and thrown into prison. But it was a chance she was willing to take.

Over the 50 years she spent in India, Amy took in hundreds of unwanted children. She became known as "Amma" or mother to them."

www.historymakers.info/inspirational-christians/amy-carmichael

INTERLUDE

Up to this point, we've talked in depth about some truly wonderful women – women who connected with Jesus in various ways but all of whom were changed or applauded because of their relationship with Jesus. And I greatly admire each of these women for different reasons. I admire:

- the Samaritan woman at the well because she kept talking with Jesus even when the topic was uncomfortable

- Mary of Bethany because of the richly intimate ways that she connected with Jesus

- The woman with the issue of blood for her faith

- Martha because she put herself out there with Jesus and made healthy adjustments to get to know Him better

- The poor widow that Jesus spotlighted for her radical generosity because in my way of thinking, she was entirely whole hearted in her devotion to God

- Mary, Jesus' mom, because as a mom, I'm touched to my very core with what it meant to look after the Son of God in a daily way

In our next chapter, we'll briefly look at some really cool women that need some recognition for how they engaged with Jesus. Getting to know each of these women provides us with some great insights in deepening our walk with Jesus!

CHAPTER 8
HONORABLE MENTIONS

We have devoted one chapter each to some very noteworthy women in Jesus life, but let's not forget some ladies who were very important, even though we don't get to know them very much. In this chapter, we'll see a few women who were interesting characters and had some really cool interactions with Jesus. Consider the following:

Mary Magdalene - dealing with crazy

All of us have "crazy" in our lives from time to time. Sometimes the crazy is kind of small and off to the side and sometimes the crazy is front and center, full stage! Jesus had his fair share of crazy that he dealt with but some of the crazy that Jesus confronted was nothing less than demonic. This can be challenging for a person to deal with who has been raised and educated in what's known as Western Civilization. The Western world doesn't give much credibility to demonic activity, unless you see some of the special effects in various horror movies. Aside from that, anything demonic gets dismissed into the crazy category and borderline ignored, which I'm convinced is exactly what the devil would like. The devil specializes in secrets, obscurity, hiding, deception, distortion, and disguise. But crazy gets front and center attention when you talk about a woman from whom seven demons were cast out. It says in Luke 8:1-2:

"Soon afterwards, He began going around from one city and village to another, proclaiming and preaching the kingdom of God. The twelve were with Him, 2 and also some women who had been healed of evil spirits and sicknesses: Mary who was called Magdalene, from whom seven demons had gone out."

If we were in Mary's shoes, we would quickly acknowledge that Jesus was the 100% best thing that ever happened to Mary. Being filled with seven demons is nothing less than sheer and utter torment, night and day, 24/7. When Mary was freed from these demons by the power of Jesus, it's no wonder that she wanted to stay around Jesus all the time. He was the author of her rescue, peace, salvation, hope, and future. Prior to His work in her life, she'd been a continual victim of demonic abuse and now in Jesus' presence, she experienced and lived in the exact opposite of demonic torment. Consequently, she's mentioned a few times in the Gospels as one of the women who travelled in the general retinue of Jesus' followers.

The next place that Mary Magadalene is mentioned is in relation to Jesus' crucifixion in John 19:25, "Therefore the soldiers did these things. But standing by the cross of Jesus were His mother, and His mother's sister, Mary the wife of Clopas, and Mary Magdalene." After

Jesus was crucified, the first person to whom Jesus reveals himself as the resurrected Christ is the former crazy lady, Mary Magdalene. Consider the following verses in John 20:1, 11-18.

1 *Now on the first day of the week Mary Magdalene came early to the tomb, while it was still dark, and saw the stone already taken away from the tomb.*

11 *But Mary was standing outside the tomb weeping; and so, as she wept, she stooped and looked into the tomb;*

12 *and she saw two angels in white sitting, one at the head and one at the feet, where the body of Jesus had been lying.*

13 *And they said to her, "Woman, why are you weeping?" She said to them, "Because they have taken away my Lord, and I do not know where they have laid Him."*

14 *When she had said this, she turned around and saw Jesus standing there, and did not know that it was Jesus.*

15 *Jesus said to her, "Woman, why are you weeping? Whom are you seeking?" Supposing Him to be the gardener, she said to Him, "Sir, if you have carried Him away, tell me where you have laid Him, and I will take Him away."*

16 *Jesus said to her, "Mary!" She turned and said to Him in Hebrew, "Rabboni!" (which means, Teacher).*

17 *Jesus said to her, "Stop clinging to Me, for I have not yet ascended to the Father; but go to My brethren and say to them, 'I ascend to My Father and your Father, and My God and your God.'"*

18 *Mary Magdalene came, announcing to the disciples, "I have seen the Lord," and that He had said these things to her.*

Take away: if you're dealing with crazy, stay close to Jesus!

Sinful woman - dealing with shame

Shame is one of the most insidious interruptions for a close relationship that has existed throughout all time. Like myself, you've probably experienced all kinds and levels of shame; from the mild embarrassment of forgetting someone's name to the unmentionable trauma you may have experienced from a personal violation. Shame is no easy burden in any situation or under any circumstance.

So consider how Jesus handled shame in Luke 7:36-50:

36 *Now one of the Pharisees was requesting Him to dine with him, and He entered the Pharisee's house and reclined at the table.* 37 *And there was a woman in the city who was a sinner; and when she learned that He was reclining at the table in the Pharisee's house, she brought an alabaster vial of perfume,* 38 *and standing behind Him at His feet, weeping, she began to wet His feet with her tears, and kept wiping them with the hair of her head, and kissing His feet and anointing them with the perfume.* 39 *Now when the Pharisee who had invited Him saw this, he said to himself, "If this man were a prophet He would know who and what sort of person this woman is who is touching Him, that she is a sinner."*

40 *Parable of Two Debtors*
And Jesus answered him, "Simon, I have something to say to you." And he replied, "Say it, Teacher." 41 *"A moneylender had two debtors: one owed five hundred denarii, and the other fifty.* 42 *"When they were unable to repay, he graciously forgave them both. So which of them will love him more?"* 43 *Simon answered and said, "I suppose the one whom he forgave more." And He said to him, "You have judged correctly."* 44 *Turning toward the woman, He said to Simon, "Do you see this woman? I entered your house; you gave Me no water for My feet, but she has wet My feet with her tears and wiped them with her*

hair. 45 *"You gave Me no kiss; but she, since the time I came in, has not ceased to kiss My feet.* 46 *"You did not anoint My head with oil, but she anointed My feet with perfume.* 47 *"For this reason I say to you, her sins, which are many, have been forgiven, for she loved much; but he who is forgiven little, loves little."* 48 *Then He said to her, "Your sins have been forgiven."* 49 *Those who were reclining at the table with Him began to say to themselves, "Who is this man who even forgives sins?"* 50 *And He said to the woman, "Your faith has saved you; go in peace."*(NASU)

Jesus contrasts Simon's disrespectful behavior with the lavish love expressed to Jesus by this sinful woman. She was forgiven much so she loved much. In contrast, Simon didn't think he needed to be forgiven much, so he loved little. But the ultimate reality for every person on the planet is that we have individually been forgiven much (with our attitudes, conversations, secret thinking, deceitful choices...). My dad used to say that none of us have nail prints in our hands, meaning that none of us are perfect. The sooner we recognize Jesus' lavish love and forgiveness to us, the quicker we will love Jesus lavishly and with opulent extravagance!

Take away: Great love is the answer to great shame.

Syrophoencian woman - dealing with insults

If you've ever been insulted, called derogatory names, or been belittled, you'll totally appreciate what happens when Jesus seems to go rogue with a woman who comes to him to heal her daughter.

In Matthew 15:21-28, we read,

Jesus went away from there, and withdrew into the district of Tyre and Sidon. 22 *And a Canaanite woman from that region came out and began to cry out, saying, "Have mercy on me, Lord, Son of David; my daughter is cruelly demon-possessed."* 23 *But He did not answer her a word. And His disciples came and implored Him, saying, "Send her away, because she keeps shouting at us."* 24 *But He answered and said, "I was sent only to the lost sheep of the house of Israel."* 25 *But she came and began to bow down before Him, saying, "Lord, help me!"* 26 *And He answered and said, "It is not good to take the children's bread and throw it to the dogs."* 27 *But she said, "Yes, Lord; but even the dogs feed on the crumbs which fall from their masters' table."* 28 *Then Jesus said to her, "O woman, your faith is great; it shall be done for you as you wish." And her daughter was healed at once.* (NASU)

This Syrophoencian woman amazes me that she doesn't get all bent out of shape, offended with Jesus and stomp off in a huff. It's the rare person that can take an insult like being called a dog, bounce back and remain persistent, but that's exactly what this lady does. She's not distracted by how Jesus' followers treat her, nor by what seems to be a derogatory cut from Jesus. She keeps her faith and focus entirely zeroed in on getting help for her daughter and because of her persistence, her daughter gets instantly healed. We can choose to be offended or we can choose to be persistent. Whatever choice we make, let's be mindful of the consequences that go with that choice.

Take away: Be more persistent than offended.

Adulterous woman - dealing with what is unfair

Our last honorable mention Jesus Chick is the woman who is caught in adultery by the religious leaders and brought to Jesus in John 8:2-11.

Early in the morning He came again into the temple, and all the people were coming to Him; and He sat down and began to teach them. 3 The scribes and the Pharisees brought a woman caught in adultery, and having set her in the center of the court, 4 they said to Him, "Teacher, this woman has been caught in adultery, in the very act. 5 "Now in the Law Moses commanded us to stone such women; what then do You say?" 6 They were saying this, testing Him, so that they might have grounds for accusing Him. But Jesus stooped down and with His finger wrote on the ground. 7 But when they persisted in asking Him, He straightened up, and said to them, "He who is without sin among you, let him be the first to throw a stone at her." 8 Again He stooped down and wrote on the ground. 9 When they heard it, they began to go out one by one, beginning with the older ones, and He was left alone, and the woman, where she was, in the center of the court. 10 Straightening up, Jesus said to her, "Woman, where are they? Did no one condemn you?" 11 She said, "No one, Lord." And Jesus said, "I do not condemn you, either. Go. From now on sin no more."

What gets under my skin about this story is that in Jewish law, both the man and woman were guilty when committing adultery and not just the woman. So why didn't the Pharisees bring the man and not just the woman? That's not a new question for Bible scholars and this question has been discussed for centuries, if not longer. So what's the deal? When we bring this to our modern living, you and I have both been on the unfair end of things at various times in our lives. Some of the unfairness has been small, but some has been massively big. Whatever the unfairness, this woman was still caught doing something wrong - so now what? I like that Jesus didn't have a knee-jerk reaction. He didn't fly off the handle and yell at the Pharisees about not bringing the man. He didn't berate the woman for breaking the law and He didn't withdraw from the whole challenge and silently slink away. Jesus held His ground, so to speak and slowly let the woman's accusers dismiss themselves as they considered His statement about being without sin. The truth is that each of us have our own failures, shortcomings, mistakes and sins. Only Jesus is perfect and He chooses to redeem rather than condemn us. Unfortunately, none of the Pharisees stayed around to connect with Jesus, but the adulterous woman received Jesus' forgiveness and restoration. In the end, she came out far superior than her accusers.

Take away: Being judgmental with others usually winds up hurting us the most.

Consider a few of the following action points that could be helpful:

- Every woman that we've read about was important. Consider how you are important to Jesus, based on a personal connection with Him.

- Dealing with shame, insults, unfairness and crazy are all very human experiences. In what ways can Jesus' presence in your life help you with these things?

- Think of a few ways that through you Jesus could help others who are struggling with shame, craziness, insults and unfairness.

SAVING MOSES®
saving babies every day

You'll notice that the proceeds of this book are donated to Saving Moses, an organization committed to saving babies ages five and under, where the need is most urgent and care is least available. We have several malnutrition clinics in Angola which provide therapeutic milk for little ones who are often hours, possibly minutes away from death due to malnutrition. Additionally, we provide NightCare in Asia for babies whose mothers are trapped in the sex industry. Our centers give these moms an alternative to bringing their babies to work or worse yet, abandoning them overnight. Instead NightCare allows them to leave their precious little ones safely in our care until morning.

We are always looking to expand our work to bring genuine love to as many babies and toddlers as we can in countries that record the highest infant mortality rates in the world! We explore opportunities for new programs in nations like Afghanistan where we can provide vaccinations and medical care in rural areas. We also invest in campaigns and special projects such as assisting with orphan babies whose parents have died from Ebola. Your purchase of this book enables us to make a difference today in the life and future of each baby we reach.

Thank you so much!!

savingmoses.org

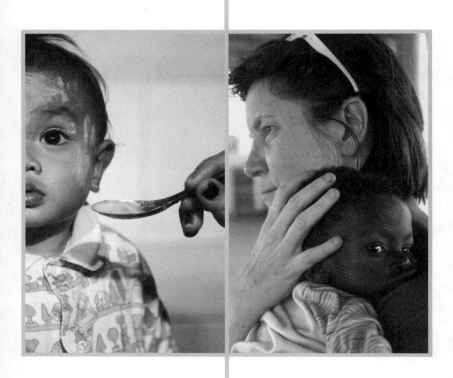

WANT TO DO MORE?

FOR ONLY $38 PER MONTH
YOU CAN BE A HERO.

Your monthly donation of $38 provides a baby either therapeutic milk at our malnutrition centers or protection and care at one of our NightCare centers.

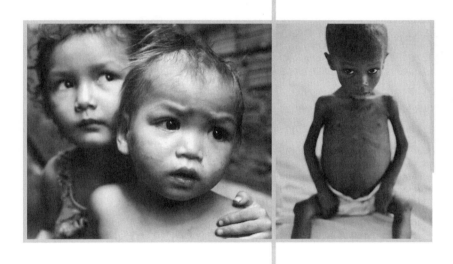

PO Box 4584 • Englewood, CO 80155-9964
1.888.637.4545 • savingmoses.org

SARAH BOWLING wants to live in a world where hugs are given in place of handshakes, conversations are face to face, and sharing a cup of coffee opens a new world of dialogue and friendship.

As an internationally recognized speaker and humanitarian, Sarah is a voice of hope for many. She is a discerning teacher of the Bible and her insights equip her to deliver authentic messages wherever she speaks, empowering her audiences to connect to the Bible in their everyday living. Sarah's Bible teaching is demonstrated in her work with *Saving Moses*, an organization committed to identifying the urgent needs for babies and toddlers around the world where the need is desperate and the help is least available. Sarah's Compassion fuels her to develop and implement the revolutionary programs established by *Saving Moses*.

Sarah leads a prolific lifestyle where genuine love isn't just projected, as in fairy tales, but expressed tangibly. When she is not enjoying a nice cup of coffee, or traveling and teaching, she is busy raising three children with her husband, Reece Bowling, the pastor of *Orchard Road Christian Center*.